Place Value Through Hundred Thousands

Write each number in standard form.

1. 6 thousand, 430

_____

2. 549 thousand, 318

_____

3. 792 thousand, 20

_____

4. three hundred sixty thousand, ten

_____

5. six hundred twenty-one thousand, five hundred

_____

6. 80,000 + 20 + 7

_____

7. 200,000 + 10,000 + 9,000 + 53

_____

Write the value of the underlined digit in short word form.

8. 1,822

_____

9. 7,603

_____

10. 25,946

_____

11. 482,509

_____

12. 941,386

_____

13. 537,460

_____

Write the number in word form, short word form, and expanded form.

14. 74,285 _____

_____

_____

Test Prep

15. The boundary line between the United States and Canada is 3,987 miles. What is the value of the digit 9?

A 9,000   **C** 90

B 900   **D** 9

16. There were 2,225 students at the Kennedy School. 100 students moved away. How many students remained? Use place value to explain your answer.

Use with text pages 4–5.

More About Place Value

Use exponents to write each number in expanded form.

1. 9,106

_____

2. 102,436

_____

Write each number in standard form.

3. $(1 \times 10^3) + (7 \times 10^2) + (8 \times 10^1) + (2 \times 10^0)$ _____

4. $(2 \times 10^4) + (8 \times 10^2) + (1 \times 10^1) + (1 \times 10^0)$ _____

5. $(3 \times 10^5) + (1 \times 10^4) + (5 \times 10^3) + (9 \times 10^1) + (2 \times 10^0)$ _____

6. $5^5 = 3,125$
$5^4 = 625$
$5^3 = 125$
$5^2 = \square$
$5^1 = \square$
$5^0 = \square$

7. $6^5 = 7,776$
$6^4 = 1,296$
$6^3 = \square$
$6^2 = \square$
$6^1 = \square$
$6^0 = \square$

8. $7^5 = 16,807$
$7^4 = 2,401$
$7^3 = \square$
$7^2 = \square$
$7^1 = \square$
$7^0 = \square$

Algebra • Equations What is the value of n in each equation?

9. $7,000 = n \times 10^3$ **10.** $n = 4 \times 3^2$ **11.** $500 = 5 \times 10^n$ **12.** $n = 9 \times 10^4$

13. Which number is equal to $(5 \times 10^5) +$
$(2 \times 10^4) + (4 \times 10^3) + (3 \times 10^1) +$
(5×10^0)?

A 524,350   **C** 52,435

B 524,035   **D** 52,350

14. There are 86,400 seconds in a day. Use
exponents to write this number in
expanded form.

_____

Use with text pages 6–7.

Place Value Through Hundred Billions

Write each number in standard form.

1. 2 million, 167 thousand, 543 _____

2. 306 billion, 425 million, 16 _____

3. five hundred billion, two hundred twelve million, forty-six thousand

   _____

4. $(2 \times 10^{10}) + (4 \times 10^9) + (8 \times 10^7) + (3 \times 10^4) + (1 \times 10^3) + (5 \times 10^0)$

   _____

Write the value of the underlined digit in short word form.

5. 4<u>5</u>6,120,781   6. 247,<u>8</u>05,392   7. 1<u>6</u>2,873,105,823

   _____   _____   _____

Write each number in expanded form using exponents.

8. 56,240,135,010   9. 87,405,203

   _____   _____

   _____   _____

   _____   _____

Solve.

10. The Pacific Ocean has an area of
    about 155,557,000 square kilometers.
    The Atlantic Ocean has an area of   _____
    about 76,762,000 square kilometers.
    Write each measurement in expanded   _____
    form using exponents.
                                                  _____

    _____

11. The value of the digit 5 is 500,000 in
    which number?

    A 51,230   **C** 125,670,689

    B 64,523,012   **D** 523,678,021

12. The world's hen population lays almost
    two billion eggs each day. Write the
    number in standard form. Explain how
    you decided how many zeros to write.

    _____

Use with text pages 8–9.

Name _____ Date _____

Compare, Order, and Round Whole Numbers

Compare. Write >, <, or = for each ◯.

1. 3,471 ◯ 3,452   **2.** 40,283 ◯ 40,567   **3.** 1,042,639 ◯ 1,042,639

4. 67,452,105 ◯ 76,021   **5.** 201,000,001 ◯ 201,002,799

Order each set of numbers from greatest to least.

6. 2,437; 2,461; 2,459   **7.** 72,390; 71,842; 79,021

Round to the place indicated by the underlined digit.

8. 7,2<u>5</u>6   **9.** 304,<u>4</u>99   **10.** 1,<u>6</u>50,000   **11.** 2<u>3</u>9,640,231

_____   _____   _____   _____

Round each number.

12. 34,781 to the nearest ten thousand   **13.** 4,362,045 to the nearest hundred thousand

_____   _____

14. 638,702,143 to the nearest million   **15.** 561,893,000 to the nearest ten million

_____   _____

Write a number for the missing digit that will make the inequality true.

16. 468,233 < 46☐,233   **17.** 45,680 > 45,6☐1   **18.** 320,124 > 320,☐24

_____   _____   _____

 **Test Prep**

19. Which comparison is false?

   A 522 < 542

   B 203,541 > 201,982

   C 561,203,758 > 561,185

   D 462,075,114 < 460,789,532

20. Round 2,460,102,000 to the nearest hundred million.

_____

4   **Use with text pages 10–12.**

Place Value Through Thousandths

Write each in standard form.

1. two hundredths _____

2. seventy-five thousandths _____

3. four hundred sixteen thousandths _____

4. twenty and three tenths _____

5. one and thirty-two hundredths _____

6. five hundred three thousandths _____

7. twelve and eleven hundredths _____

8. two hundred fourteen thousandths _____

Write each decimal in words.

9. 0.52

10. 0.023

11. 0.408

_____

_____

_____

12. 10.3

13. 2.014

14. 8.21

_____

_____

_____

Write the value of the underlined digit in words.

15. 34.1<u>2</u>

16. 10.16<u>4</u>

17. 5.<u>7</u>82

_____

_____

_____

Test Prep

18. Which underlined digit has the value four hundredths?

   A 20.<u>4</u>53   C 2.3<u>4</u>8

   B <u>4</u>36.72   D 1.00<u>4</u>

19. Oak trees grow 0.055 inches a day. Write the decimal in words.

_____

Use with text pages 14–15.

Problem-Solving Strategy: Find a Pattern

Use a pattern to solve Problems 1–3.

Patty earned $8.50 for the first week she worked. She earned $10.00 and $11.50 for the next two weeks she worked.

Patty's Earnings				
Week 1	Week 2	Week 3	Week 4	Week 5
$8.50	$10.00	$11.50	?	?

Show Your Work

1. How much will Patty earn at her part-time job in Week 4?

   _____

2. How much will Patty earn at her part-time job in Week 5?

   _____

3. What will Patty's total earnings be after 7 weeks of part-time work? Explain.

   _____

   _____

4. A tomato plant is 10 in. tall when it is planted. It grows to 13 in. tall after one week. The plant is 16 in. tall after two weeks. It grows to 19 in. tall after three weeks. If the tomato plant continues to grow at this rate, how tall will it be after five weeks?

   _____

5. If the tomato plant continues to grow at this rate, how tall will it be after eight weeks?

   _____

Use with text pages 16–18.

Compare, Order, and Round Decimals

Compare. Write >, <, or = for each ◯.

1. 0.24 ◯ 0.18 **2.** 0.45 ◯ 0.450 **3.** 0.702 ◯ 0.701 **4.** 0.063 ◯ 0.63

5. 3.682 ◯ 3.679 **6.** 42 ◯ 41.99 **7.** 4.926 ◯ 5.1 **8.** 8.001 ◯ 8.1

Order the numbers from greatest to least.

9. 5.63; 0.563; 5 **10.** 0.21; 21; 0.2 **11.** 38.41; 3.842; 3.843

_____ _____ _____

Round to the place of the underlined digit.

12. <u>3</u>.099 _____ **13.** 0.2<u>68</u> _____ **14.** 6.<u>2</u>53 _____ **15.** 9.<u>9</u>72 _____

Round each number.

16. 6.027 to the nearest hundredth _____

17. 5.071 to the nearest tenth _____

Algebra • Properties Compare. Write >, <, or = for each ◯, given a = 0.556, b = 0.56, c = 0.056, d = 0.1

18. a ◯ b **19.** c ◯ d **20.** b ◯ c **21.** d ◯ a

_____ _____ _____ _____

Find the missing digit that will make the inequality true.

22. 0.45 > 0.☐9 **23.** 0.☐93 < 0.636 **24.** 4.238 > 4.23☐

_____ _____ _____

25. Which decimal is greater than 17.483?

   A 17.099 C 17.438

   B 17.384 D 17.504

26. On Monday Oscar's kitten weighed 2.567 pounds. On Friday he weighed 2.561 pounds. On Sunday he weighed 2.57 pounds. When did he weigh the most?

_____

Use with text pages 20–22.

Expressions and Addition Properties

Write an algebraic expression for each word phrase.

1. take 2 from a number _____

2. 8 more than a number _____

3. add 13 to a number _____

4. 10 is decreased by a number _____

5. subtract 6 from a number _____

6. 5 plus a number _____

7. 7 is decreased by a number _____

8. 3 more than a number _____

Translate each algebraic expression into words.

9. $a + 6$ _____

10. $10 - x$ _____

11. $7 + n$ _____

12. $y - 4$ _____

13. $m - 17$ _____

14. $5 - t$ _____

15. $9 + b$ _____

16. $k + 6$ _____

17. $x + 3$ _____

18. $12 - p$ _____

Evaluate each expression when $n = 12$. Then write $>$, $<$, or $=$ to compare the expressions.

19. $n + 0 \bigcirc n - 4$

20. $n + 7 \bigcirc 7 + n$

21. $(n + 3) + 8 \bigcirc n + (3 + 8)$

22. $n - 10 \bigcirc 15 - n$

Test Prep

23. Rachel has $7. Josiah has more money than Rachel. Leah has $2.00 more than Josiah. Which expression shows how much money Leah has, if j represents how much more money Josiah has than Rachel?

    A $7 - 2 + j$ **C** $7 + j - 2$

    B $7 + j + 2$ **D** $7 - j + 2$

24. According to an old story, all the tigers in the world came from Mt. In-Wang in Korea. Suppose there were 450 tigers on Mt. In-Wang one year. The next year there were more. Write an algebraic expression to show the number of tigers the second year. Explain what the variable represents.

    _____

Use with text pages 28–30.

Estimate Sums and Differences

Estimate. Tell which method you used.

1. 379 +379	2. 651 −214	3. 538 +583	4. 790 +928
5. 738 −458	6. 206 +669	7. 177 +782	8. 546 −212
9. 9,009 +3,924	10. 7,487 −1,234	11. 3,182 +2,982	12. 6,756 −4,809
13. 66,045 +23,413	14. 24,800 −22,765	15. 19,210 +52,512	16. 81,999 −38,700

17. 46,469 − 2,942

_____

18. $42 + $65 + $23

_____

19. $49 + $17

_____

20. 4,073 + 2,987 + 12,460

_____

21. $13 + $6 + $7 + $2

_____

22. $254 + $982 + $402

_____

Estimate. Decide whether the sum is closer to 100 or 200.

23. 78 + 83   24. $94 + $54   25. $67 + $65   26. 112 + 49

_____ _____ _____ _____

Test Prep

27. On their Arizona holiday, the Santos family spent $387 on gas, $245 on food, $112 on tickets, and $78 on souvenirs. What is a reasonable estimated range for the total amount they spent?

A $400–$600   C $600–$1,000

B $500–$700   D $600–$700

28. Mr. MacGregor's garden produced 113 tomatoes one week, 246 the next week, 287 the third week, and 366 the fourth week. About how many tomatoes did his garden produce over those four weeks? Explain your estimate.

_____

9

Use with text pages 32–33.

Add and Subtract Whole Numbers

Add or subtract. Check that your answer is reasonable.

1. $\begin{array}{r} 765 \\ +195 \end{array}$
2. $\begin{array}{r} 907 \\ -614 \end{array}$
3. $\begin{array}{r} 249 \\ -187 \end{array}$
4. $\begin{array}{r} 777 \\ +555 \end{array}$

5. $\begin{array}{r} 972 \\ -582 \end{array}$
6. $\begin{array}{r} 810 \\ +312 \end{array}$
7. $\begin{array}{r} 631 \\ +299 \end{array}$
8. $\begin{array}{r} 407 \\ -324 \end{array}$

9. $\begin{array}{r} 2,653 \\ +\ \ 466 \end{array}$
10. $\begin{array}{r} 8,741 \\ +1,199 \end{array}$
11. $\begin{array}{r} 4,908 \\ -\ \ 89 \end{array}$
12. $\begin{array}{r} 9,001 \\ -5,764 \end{array}$

13. $\begin{array}{r} 14,886 \\ -\ 9,902 \end{array}$
14. $\begin{array}{r} 63,337 \\ +21,068 \end{array}$
15. $\begin{array}{r} 80,015 \\ -\ \ 246 \end{array}$
16. $\begin{array}{r} 42,769 \\ -15,823 \end{array}$

17. $5,008 - 1,867$
18. $6,566 + 791$
19. $429 + 6,846 + 17,707$

20. $8,698 + 4,589$
21. $7,330 - 854$
22. $32,787 + 27,998 + 40,222$

Algebra • Patterns Find each sum or difference when $a = 100,000$ and $b = 799$.

23. $a - 4$
24. $33,000 + a$
25. $a + 400,000$
26. $a - b$

Test Prep

27. The Rogun Dam is 1,066 feet high. The Nurek Dam, which was built five years earlier, is 984 feet high. How much higher is the Rogun Dam than the Nurek Dam?

    A 2,050 ft   C 82 ft

    B 182 ft   D 72 ft

28. Mr. Rosa's new carpet business, made $234 on Monday, $452 on Tuesday, $1,609 on Wednesday, $567 on Thursday, and $973 on Friday. Over the same five days, his competitor made $4,206. How much more did his competitor make than Mr. Rosa?

Use with text pages 34–36.

Add and Subtract Greater Numbers

Add or subtract. Tell which method you used.

1. 785,928
    +216,904

2. 862,094
    − 74,198

3. 4,710,008
    +2,333,456

4. 301,776
    −200,000

5. 9,663,281
    −7,600,000

6. 432,986
    − 66,454

7. 2,010,838
    + 500,010

8. 198,519
    + 67,834

9. 6,000,000
    −3,560,714

10. 990,374
    +613,694

11. 8,888,123
    + 24,002

12. 1,112,738
    −1,054,628

13. 3,456,654
    −2,567,765

14. 8,608,086
    − 543,892

15. 5,491,207
    +1,090,000

16. 32,087,111
    + 4,922,843

17. 265,000 + 140,000

18. 100,000 − 24,700

19. 2,864,700 − 2,643,200

_____

_____

_____

20. 7,778,673 − 4,211,002

21. 2,880,199 + 3,857,735

22. 14,832,645 − 3,293,001

_____

_____

_____

Test Prep

23. City A has a population of 3,224,678.
    City B is home to 113,870 people. City C
    has a 738,645 residents. How many
    more people live in City A than in City B
    and City C combined?

    A 3,110,808   **C** 2,372,163

    B 2,486,033   **D** 2,129,653

24. The Sun is an average distance of
    92,960,000 miles away from the Earth.
    The Moon is an average distance of
    238,900 miles away from the Earth.
    If the Moon is directly between the
    Earth and the Sun, what is the average
    distance from the Moon to the Sun?

    _____

Use with text pages 38–39.

Addition and Subtraction Equations

Write the equation shown by the model. Then solve the equation.

1.

games played: 22	
won: 17	lost: a

_____

_____

2.

a	
5	23

_____

_____

Use mental math to solve the equations. Use models if necessary.

3. $a - 6 = 10$ **4.** $4 + x = 7$ **5.** $20 - c = 16$ **6.** $s + 25 = 30$

_____   _____   _____   _____

7. $3 + y = 4$ **8.** $100 - m = 86$ **9.** $k + 17 = 19$ **10.** $q + \$3 = \$4$

_____   _____   _____   _____

11. $50 - r = 47$ **12.** $12 + b = 16$ **13.** $n - 25 = 25$ **14.** $t - 7 = 82$

_____   _____   _____   _____

15. $x + 15 = 30$ **16.** $y - 95 = 5$ **17.** $75 + s = 85$ **18.** $\$17 - c = \$5$

_____   _____   _____   _____

19. $33 + m = 44$ **20.** $16 - k = 1$ **21.** $q + 27 = 27$ **22.** $n - 14 = 100$

_____   _____   _____   _____

Test Prep

23. Becca is running a 26-mile marathon. She has just reached the 14-mile mark. Which of the following equations would help you find out how many miles she has already run?

A $m - 14 = 26$ **C** $14 - m = 26$

B $26 + 14 = m$ **D** $m + 14 = 26$

24. Nicolai and his mother climbed Mt. Katahdin. His mother was the first hiker to reach the top. She got there in 4 hours and 25 minutes. If there was 15 minutes between their arrivals, how long did the climb take Nicolai?

_____

Use with text pages 40–41.

Problem-Solving Decision:
Relevant Information

Draw a model to solve. If there is not enough information, tell what information is needed.

Show Your Work

1. Vicky and Sean plan to make a surprise dessert. They have $15.00 to buy key limes, condensed milk, eggs, whipped cream, and a graham cracker pie crust. The pie crust costs $2.39. Do they have enough money to buy the other ingredients?

_____

_____

2. When they go to the supermarket they see some pretzels for $.99 they'd like to buy. Sean has some change in his pocket. Can he buy the pretzels?

_____

_____

3. Vicky and Sean need to mix together 4 ounces of key lime juice, 8 ounces of condensed milk and the eggs. How many ounces are in that mixture?

_____

_____

4. Vicky and Sean decide to buy special plates, napkins and forks in which to serve the dessert. They spend $5.50 for these. Could they pay for these with the change left over from the supermarket?

_____

_____

5. According to the recipe, there are 8 servings of dessert. If Vicky, Sean, their parents and 3 sisters all have a serving, will there be any left?

_____

Use with text pages 42–43.

Expressions and Multiplication Properties

Write an expression for each.

1. a number multiplied by 6 _____

2. a number added to 57 _____

3. 64 divided by a number _____

4. 84 decreased by a number _____

5. the product of a number and 12 _____

6. a number divided by 17 _____

Evaluate. Tell which property you used.

7. $2 \times 56 \times 5$

_____

8. $50 \times (2 \times 78)$

_____

9. $3 \times 12 \times 0$

_____

10. $3 \times 1 \times 20$

_____

11. $50(34 \times 20)$

_____

12. $(43 \times 16) \times 0$

_____

Evaluate each expression, given $n = 2$, $r = 5$, and $s = 6$.

13. $4s$

_____

14. $3 \times (n \cdot r)$

_____

15. $120 - r$

_____

16. $n + r - s$

_____

17. $(4 + 6) \times s$

_____

18. $7(n \times r) \times 1$

_____

19. $n(s \times r)$

_____

20. $(56 \times s) \times 0$

_____

Test Prep

21. Given that $x = 4$, $y = 13$, and $z = 25$, which expression equals 1,300?

   A $(x + 6) \times z$ C $(13 - y) \times x \times z$

   B $(x \times z) + 13$ D xyz

22. Give an example showing the use of the Associative Property of Multiplication.

_____

_____

Use with text pages 60–61.

Model the Distributive Property

Use the Distributive Property to multiply. Show the partial products for each and find the sum. Then write a multiplication sentence for each.

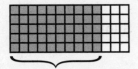

1. 5 × 13 _____

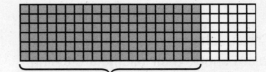

2. 6 × 26 _____

**Draw and divide a rectangle to show each product.
Use the Distributive Property to find the product.**

3. 4 × 24

_____

4. 6 × 12

_____

5. 8 × 43

_____

6. 7 × 36

_____

Test Prep

7. Which shows the correct use of the Distributive Property to find the product 8 × 73?

   A (8 × 70) × (8 × 3)

   B (8 + 70) × (8 + 3)

   C (8 × 70) + (8 × 3)

   D 8 + (70 × 3)

8. Show how to use the Distributive Property to find the product of 9 × 73.

_____

_____

Use with text pages 62–63.

Problem-Solving Strategy:
Use Logical Reasoning

Use logical reasoning to solve each problem.

Show Your Work

1. Caren, John, Ty, and Rhianna are in a talent show. Their talents are telling a poem, playing the banjo, playing the guitar, and singing. Caren tells a poem. John does not play the banjo. Rhianna plays guitar. What talent does Ty perform?

   _____

2. Mary, Rhea, Susan, and Joanne sing 1 part in a harmony group. Joanne sings the lowest part, and Rhea does not sing the highest part. Susan sings the second lowest part. Who sings the second highest part?

   _____

3. Four students are standing in line offstage, waiting to perform. Steven is directly in front of Larry. Jose is directly behind Aiko. Larry was the last person to get in line. In what order are the students standing?

   _____

4. Mrs. Jameson, Mr. Thomas, and Ms. O'Rourke are sitting in seats numbered 18-A, 18-B, and 18-C as they watch their children perform. Neither Mr. Thomas or Ms. O'Rourke are sitting in seat 18-A. Ms. O'Rourke is sitting next to Mrs. Jameson. In which seat is each person?

   _____

Use with text pages 64–66.

Multiply by One-Digit Numbers

Find the product.

1. $\begin{array}{r} 79 \\ \times\ 8 \\ \hline \end{array}$

2. $\begin{array}{r} 43 \\ \times\ 7 \\ \hline \end{array}$

3. $\begin{array}{r} 564 \\ \times\ 6 \\ \hline \end{array}$

4. $\begin{array}{r} 972 \\ \times\ 4 \\ \hline \end{array}$

5. 4×59

6. 862×7

7. $9 \times 8{,}720$

8. $721{,}053 \times 4$

Algebra • Functions Copy and complete each function table.

9.

Rule: $y = 3x$				
x	138	497	2,855	4,622
y				

10.

Rule: $y = 9x$				
x	138	497	2,850	4,622
y				

Use the Distributive Property to rewrite each expression. Then solve.

11. 5×680

12. $4 \times 91{,}585$

Algebra • Expressions Evaluate each expression when $a = 9$, $b = 37$, $c = 729$, and $d = 8{,}610$.

13. $4 \times c$

14. $3b \times a$

15. $7(a \times d)$

16. $3 \times (d \times b)$

Test Prep

17. The bookstore received a delivery of 8 boxes. Each box contained 65 books. Nine books were damaged and returned. How many books did the bookstore keep?

A 520

C 480

B 511

D 471

18. How can you use the Distributive Property to find the product of 5 and 6,723?

_____

Use with text pages 68–70.

Patterns in Multiples of 10

Use a pattern or mental math to find each product.

1. 60 × 7	**2.** 40 × 4	**3.** 50 × 9	**4.** 600 × 3
5. 700 × 8	**6.** 900 × 6	**7.** 400 × 8	**8.** 6,000 × 7
9. 3,000 × 4	**10.** 9,000 × 9	**11.** 7,000 × 5	**12.** 8,000 × 3

13. 70 × 40   **14.** 600 × 50   **15.** 80 × 80   **16.** 3,000 × 70

_____   _____   _____   _____

17. 80 × 900   **18.** 800 × 70   **19.** 60 × 7,000   **20.** 8,000 × 90

_____   _____   _____   _____

Multiply.

21. 38 × 20   **22.** 53 × 40   **23.** 75 × 70   **24.** 98 × 40

_____   _____   _____   _____

25. 172 × 20   **26.** 307 × 50   **27.** 529 × 80   **28.** 910 × 70

_____   _____   _____   _____

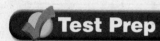 **Test Prep**

29. What is the product of 6,000 × 9,000?

   A 54,000   **C** 5,400,000

   B 540,000   **D** 54,000,000

30. How can you use multiplying by tens to find the product of 82 × 40?

_____

Use with text pages 72–73.

Estimate Products

Estimate by using front-end estimation. Then estimate by rounding.

1. 43 × 67

2. 35 × 78

3. 62 × 81

4. 58 × 96

_____ _____ _____ _____

5. 742 × 33

6. 81 × 487

7. 312 × 69

8. 156 × 48

_____ _____ _____ _____

9. 87 × 635

10. 78 × 873

11. 12 × 925

12. 46 × 607

_____ _____ _____ _____

Estimate. Give a range which includes the actual product.

13. 27 × 39

14. 56 × 32

15. 99 × 14

16. 48 × 61

_____ _____ _____ _____

17. 85 × 317

18. 56 × 618

19. 29 × 888

20. 409 × 755

_____ _____ _____ _____

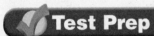 **Test Prep** ════════════════════════════

21. What is the best estimate of 824 × 78?

    A 52,000   **C** 64,000

    B 56,000   **D** 72,000

22. Quan has $1,500. He wants to buy 32 prints for his art store. He must pay $55 for each print. Does Quan have enough money to buy all the prints he wants? Use estimation to explain your answer.

_____

Use with text pages 74–75.

Multiply by Two-Digit Numbers

Find each product. Estimate or use a calculator to check.

1. $\begin{array}{r} 72 \\ \times\,13 \\ \hline \end{array}$

2. $\begin{array}{r} 45 \\ \times\,18 \\ \hline \end{array}$

3. $\begin{array}{r} 113 \\ \times\,42 \\ \hline \end{array}$

4. 32×74

5. 62×78

6. 44×617

7. 983×48

_____   _____   _____   _____

Use the Distributive Property to rewrite each expression. Then evaluate.

8. 38×25

9. 51×413

10. 67×704

_____   _____   _____

Algebra • Expressions Evaluate each expression, when $j = 5$, $k = 20$, and $l = 100$.

11. $50k$

12. $582 \times l$

13. $4(j \times j)$

14. $l \times (4 \times j)$

15. $(32 \times k)j$

_____   _____   _____   _____   _____

Evaluate each expression.

16. $56 \times p$, when $p = 42$ _____

17. $36s$, when $s = 102$ _____

18. $9c \cdot d$, when $c = 21$ and $d = 8$

19. $(e \cdot f) \cdot g$, when $e = 3$, $f = 42$, $g = 22$

_____

_____

Test Prep

20. The Riverside Dance Theater sold 456 tickets for a ballet performance. Each ticket cost $29. How much money did the theater collect?

   A $13,324   C $12,224

   B $13,224   D $12,214

21. The Riverside Dance Theater has 47 members in its dance troupe. Each member sold 75 tickets last season. Write an equation showing how many tickets each member sold. Solve.

   _____

Use with text pages 76–78.

Problem-Solving Decision:
Explain Your Solution

Solve Problems 1–5. Explain your answers.

Show Your Work

1. Your class is taking a trip to Washington, D.C., which is 589 miles from your town. If the bus driver travels 245 miles each day, will you complete the trip in 2 days?

_____

2. Frank has brought $38 to spend on souvenirs. Janice has brought $18 to spend. Does Frank have more than twice as much money as Janice?

_____

3. Paulo is collecting postcards from famous places in Washington, D.C. He wants to buy 59 postcards. He can buy 5 postcards for $1. He has $13. Does he have enough money to buy the postcards he wants?

_____

4. Your teacher has bought juice drinks for 48 students to drink on the bus ride. He bought 7 packs of boxed drinks. There are 8 drinks in each pack. If every student has a drink, will there be enough for your teacher to have one?

_____

5. When you return from the trip, you will write a report about it. You have been asked to write a 575-word report. You can fit 275 words on each page. How many pages will your report be?

_____

Use with text pages 80–81.

Name _____ Date _____

Estimate Quotients

Estimate the quotient.

1. 6)193

2. 5)439

3. 9)3,621

4. 7)4,310

_____

_____

5. 8)78,452

6. 5)22,801

7. 5)266,113

8. 7)442,597

_____

_____

9. 322 ÷ 6

10. 507 ÷ 4

11. 6,828 ÷ 9

12. 3,412 ÷ 5

_____

_____

13. 12,461 ÷ 7

14. 65,135 ÷ 8

15. 588,117 ÷ 6

16. 528,117 ÷ 9

_____

_____

Test Prep

17. Luanne had 239 crafts to arrange as evenly as she could on 8 display tables. Which of these is a reasonable estimate of the number of crafts she put on each table?

A 3 crafts   **C** 300 crafts

B 30 crafts   **D** 3,000 crafts

18. Jodie had 178 crafts to arrange on 8 display tables. Estimate how many she should put on each table to arrange them as evenly as possible. Tell what numbers you used for the dividend and the divisor.

_____

Use with text pages 86–87.

One-Digit Divisors

Divide and check.

1. $7\overline{)641}$

2. $5\overline{)475}$

3. $4\overline{)2{,}979}$

4. $5\overline{)82{,}345}$

5. $8\overline{)73{,}691}$

6. $7\overline{)862{,}715}$

7. $728 \div 6$

8. $568 \div 4$

9. $7{,}324 \div 2$

_____

_____

_____

10. $23{,}456 \div 8$

11. $74{,}114 \div 9$

12. $217{,}422 \div 4$

_____

_____

_____

Algebra • Equations The division statement $16 \div 5 = 3$ R1 can be written as $(5 \times 3) + 1 = 16$. Write and solve a division statement for each equation.

13. $4a + r = 19$

14. $5a + r = 33$

15. $6a + r = 19$

Test Prep

16. Al works in a nursery. He plants 486 seedlings in rows. He plants 9 seedlings in each row. Which answer shows how many rows he plants?

    A 34 rows

    C 54 rows

    B 46 rows

    D 62 rows

17. Al plants 335 rose bushes. He plants 8 in each row. How many full rows does he plant? How many rose bushes are in the last row?

    _____

Use with text pages 88–89.

Name _____   Date _____

Problem-Solving Application: Use Operations

Use the table for Problems 1–5. Name the operation(s) you used.

Mrs. Monroe's Vegetable Garden		
Plant	Number of Plants	Selling Cost
Tomatoes	20	$1 each
Lettuce	14	$3 each
Carrots	22	$3/bunch
Celery	16	$2/bunch
Peppers	48	$1 each

Show Your Work

1. How many tomato and lettuce plants does Mrs. Monroe have?

_____

2. How many plants does Mrs. Monroe have that are not peppers?

_____

3. If Mrs. Monroe opens up a vegetable stand and sells 37 peppers, how much money will she earn?

_____

4. Will Mrs. Monroe make more money if she sells 15 bunches of celery, or if she sells 13 bunches of carrots? Explain.

_____

5. Next year, Mrs. Monroe plans to have the same total number of plants but an equal number of each kind of plant. How many of each plant will she have?

_____

24

Use with text pages 90–91.

Divisibility

Tell whether each number is divisible by 2, 3, 4, 5, 6, 9, or 10.

1. 633

2. 218

3. 850

4. 720

_____

_____

5. 555

6. 216

7. 673

8. 1,786

_____

_____

9. 5,944

10. 7,236

11. 6,200

12. 6,480

_____

_____

Algebra • Expressions Find a value of *n* that makes the expression divisible by 2, 4, and 9.

13. 12*n*

14. *n* + 8

15. 10*n*

16. *n* − 12

_____

Test Prep

17. Which number is divisible by 2, 3, 6, and 9?

   A 132   **C** 234

   B 134   **D** 235

18. Alicia has 148 red beads. Out of the multiples of 2, 3, 4, 5, 6, 9, and 10, what is the greatest number of red beads she can string on necklaces and have no red beads left over?

_____

Use with text pages 92–94.

Zeros in the Quotient

Divide and check.

1. 4)241

2. 7)725

3. 9)2,748

4. 7)45,504

5. 6)62,432

6. 8)336,242

7. 721 ÷ 4

8. 203 ÷ 8

9. 9,020 ÷ 9

_____

_____

_____

10. 7,201 ÷ 6

11. 60,800 ÷ 8

12. 43,024 ÷ 5

_____

_____

_____

13. 34,007 ÷ 5

14. 144,368 ÷ 9

15. 752,013 ÷ 5

_____

_____

_____

Test Prep

16. Elise has 2,432 shells divided evenly into 8 jars. How many shells are in each jar?

   A 34 shells   C 304 shells

   B 300 shells   D 340 shells

17. Eric paid $840 for 6 antique rings. Each ring cost the same amount. How much did each ring cost?

   _____

Use with text pages 96–97.

Problem-Solving Strategy:
Guess and Check

Use Guess and Check to solve each problem.

Show Your Work

1. The school had a carnival to raise money. A group of 11 students bought either hot dogs for $1.00 each or hamburgers for $2.00 each. The total amount they spent was $18.00. How many hot dogs and hamburgers did they buy?

   _____

2. The sixth grade made $32 at a cake sale. They received only $10, $5, and $1 bills and collected a total of 7 bills. What combination of bills did they receive?

   _____

3. Three students came to the bake sale to shop. The sum of their ages is 33. The product of their ages is 1,320. How old are they?

   _____

4. Carla made 20 necklaces and bracelets to sell at the carnival. She made 4 more bracelets than necklaces. How many bracelets and necklaces did Carla make?

   _____

5. The baked goods are set up on a table that is 3 times as long as it is wide. The perimeter is 256 inches. How wide is the table?

   _____

Use with text pages 98–100.

Solve Equations

Solve each problem.

1. At the paperback book convention, Lucia sold 6 of the same kind of book for $54. How much did she sell each book for?
6n = 54

54					
n	n	n	n	n	n

_____

2. Lucia displayed 24 books in 4 rows. She had the same number of books in each row. How many books were in each row?
24 ÷ n = 4

24			
n	n	n	n

_____

Use mental math to solve the equations.

3. $3t = 27$ 4. $7s = 35$ 5. $81 \div y = 9$ 6. $56 \div p = 7$

_____   _____   _____   _____

Algebra • Equations Replace *n* with 6. Is the equation true? Write *yes* or *no*.

7. $4n = 24$ 8. $12 \div n = 3$ 9. $30 \div n = 5$ 10. $7n = 42$

_____   _____   _____   _____

Use the function rule to find each value of *y*.

11. Rule: $y = 24 \div x$

y	2	4	6	8
x				

12. $y = 4x$

x	2	4	6	9
y				

Test Prep

13. Lori gave each of her 2 brothers the same number of crackers. She gave them 8 crackers in all. How many did she give each brother?

   A 2 crackers   C 8 crackers

   B 4 crackers   D 16 crackers

14. Pete's Stationery sells notebooks for $9 each. James purchased $54 worth of notebooks. How many notebooks did he buy?

_____

Use with text pages 102–104.

Divide by Multiples of 10, 100, and 1,000

Divide. Use patterns, basic facts, or multiples of 10.

1. $360 \div 9$

_____

2. $480 \div 60$

_____

3. $21,000 \div 300$

_____

4. $56,000 \div 80$

_____

5. $28,000 \div 7,000$

_____

6. $45,000 \div 500$

_____

7. $160,000 \div 8,000$

_____

8. $240,000 \div 4,000$

_____

9. $400,000 \div 5,000$

_____

10. $50\overline{)4,500}$

_____

11. $200\overline{)800,000}$

_____

12. $3,000\overline{)900,000}$

_____

Use compatible numbers and multiples of 10 to estimate each quotient.

13. $4,280 \div 60$

_____

14. $23,600 \div 400$

_____

15. $17,500 \div 92$

_____

16. $78,000 \div 425$

_____

17. $412,000 \div 380$

_____

18. $655,000 \div 820$

_____

Test Prep

19. Which is the best estimate of 53,500 divided by 62?

A 9   **C** 900

B 90   **D** 9,000

20. Use compatible numbers and multiples of 10 to estimate $31,200 \div 83$. Show the compatible numbers you used.

_____

Use with text pages 110–111.

Two-Digit Divisors

Divide. Check your answer.

1. $30\overline{)95}$

2. $16\overline{)73}$

3. $22\overline{)89}$

4. $27\overline{)81}$

5. $18\overline{)56}$

6. $22\overline{)836}$

7. $31\overline{)938}$

8. $42\overline{)849}$

9. $84\overline{)512}$

10. $96 \div 12$

11. $460 \div 65$

12. $825 \div 25$

_____

_____

_____

13. $770 \div 38$

14. $635 \div 21$

15. $774 \div 18$

_____

_____

_____

Test Prep

16. Tammy works in a bookstore. There are 896 books to be packed into crates. Tammy packs 128 books into one large crate. The small crates will hold 64 books each. How many small crates will Tammy need?

A 12   **C** 120

B 14   **D** 140

17. Tammy is stacking 412 books on shelves. She can stack 24 books on each shelf. How many shelves will she fill? Will she have any books left over? If so, how many books will she have left over?

_____

Use with text pages 112–113.

Problem-Solving Strategy: Work Backward

Work backward to solve each problem.

1. Your basketball coach is retiring, and you are saving money to buy her a gift. The gift will cost $33. If you save $5 per week for the next 4 weeks, you will have enough to buy the gift. How much money did you already have?

_____

2. Tamyra buys some school supplies at the store. She buys 2 notebooks that cost $5 each and 4 pens that cost $3.00 all together. She ends up with $2 change in her pocket. How much money did Tamyra have before she bought her school supplies?

_____

3. Joyce paid $3 more for her hat than Jen paid for her scarf. Jen paid $1 less for her scarf than Kisha paid for her shirt. Kisha paid $18 for her shirt. How much did Joyce spend for her hat?

_____

4. At a school, there were 32 more fifth-graders than fourth-graders. There were 12 fewer fourth-graders than third-graders. If there were 96 third-graders at the school, how many fifth-graders were there?

_____

Use with text pages 114–116.

Adjusting Quotients

Divide. Check your answers.

1. 32)250

2. 17)512

3. 24)210

4. 56)521

5. 42)308

6. 72)649

7. 34)544

8. 31)188

9. 92)472

10. 55)311

11. 63)448

12. 28)170

13. 726 ÷ 32

14. 519 ÷ 74

15. 925 ÷ 29

16. 242 ÷ 32

_____   _____   _____   _____

Algebra • Functions Complete the table or rule.

17. Rule: Divide by 10.

Input	Output
100	_____
200	_____
260	_____
520	_____

18. Rule: Divide by 15.

Input	Output
75	_____
_____	10
225	_____
_____	30

19. Rule: _____

Input	Output
96	8
120	10
240	20
264	22

Test Prep

20. An electric hybrid car travels 612 miles. It uses 12 gallons of gas. How many miles per gallon does the car get?

A 601

B 501

C 61

D 51

21. A regular car gets 32 miles per gallon. If it travels 608 miles, how many gallons of gas does it use?

_____

Use with text pages 118–119.

Division With Greater Numbers

Divide and check.

1. $24\overline{)7,230}$

2. $18\overline{)3,450}$

3. $72\overline{)7,368}$

4. $37\overline{)8,023}$

5. $82\overline{)55,362}$

6. $24\overline{)18,095}$

7. $4,233 \div 11$

8. $9,721 \div 58$

_____

_____

9. $12,480 \div 51$

10. $387,422 \div 16$

_____

_____

Algebra • Equations If q is the quotient and r is the remainder, write and solve a division problem for each equation.

11. $36q + r = 2,599$

12. $12q + r = 448$

Test Prep

13. Louisa earns $48,880 a year. There are 52 weeks in a year. How much does she earn a week?

A $94   **C** $940

B $840   **D** $1,040

14. Find $72,450 \div 85$. Show how to check your work.

_____

Use with text pages 120–122.

Order of Operations

Simplify.

1. $(20 - 2) \div 3$

2. $4 + (8 - 2) \times 5$

3. $6 + (2 \times 6) \div 2^2$

_____

_____

_____

4. $(19 + 2) \div (9 - 2) \times 4$

5. $(3^2 - 6) \times (10 + 5)$

6. $4 + (6 \times 2) - 7$

_____

_____

_____

7. $135 - 3 - (4 \times 12) + 16$

8. $(9 - 5)^2 - (6 - 2) \times 3$

9. $1{,}634 + (14 \times 2) \div 2^2$

_____

_____

_____

Write >, <, or = for each $\bigcirc$.

10. $22 + (16 - 8) \bigcirc (22 + 16) - 8$

11. $32 + (4 \times 2) \bigcirc (32 + 4) \times 2$

12. $(36 \div 4) - 3^2 \bigcirc 16 - (3 \times 4)$

13. $(12 \times 3) + 2^2 \bigcirc (18 \div 3)^2 + 8$

14. $2{,}578 + (456 - 12) \bigcirc (2{,}578 + 456) - 12$

15. $(3^2 - 4) \times 8 \bigcirc (18 + 2) + 2^2 \times 2$

Mental Math   Use mental math to simplify.

16. $5 + (8 - 2) - 6$ _____

17. $(12 - 2) + (5 + 5) + (6 + 4)$ _____

18. $8 + 18 - (4 \times 2)$ _____

19. $(7 \div 7) \times (8 \div 8) \times (9 \div 9)$ _____

Algebra • Expressions   Evaluate the expression, given $x = 3$ and $y = 7$.

20. $(x + y)^2$ _____

21. $(2x + 6y) \div x$ _____

22. Which answer shows the expression $44 + 12 \div 2 - 2^2 \times 2$ correctly simplified using the order of operations?

   A 20   **C** 42

   B 24   **D** 48

23. Rewrite the expression $28 - 3 \times 4 + 3^2$. Put in parentheses to show the correct order of operations. Simplify the expression.

   _____

Use with text pages 124–126.

Problem-Solving Application:
Interpret Remainders

Solve. Explain how you decided to interpret each remainder.

Show Your Work

1. Your school is having an arts day. There are 178 students who will attend, and a maximum of 15 students can work in each room. How many rooms will you need?

_____

_____

2. The 178 students have a choice of art projects. They can choose painting, drawing, sculpture, weaving, or paper-making. If the painting project can have extra students, but the other projects must have an equal number of students, how many students will be working on the painting project?

_____

_____

3. In one room of 15 students, there are 9 boxes of charcoal for drawing. How many additional boxes are needed?

_____

_____

4. In the weaving class, George is making placemats to use in the cafeteria. He started at 12:00 P.M., and he hopes to make 20 by the end of the arts day at 6:00 P.M. How many placemats does he need to make per hour to reach his goal?

_____

_____

5. One box of charcoal for drawing costs $2. Jen has $11. How many boxes of charcoal can she buy?

_____

_____

Measurement Concepts

Decide what unit of measure to use. Then measure each item.

1. the length of a chapter book _____

2. the width of a chapter book _____

3. the height of a chair _____

4. the length of a pair of scissors _____

5. the length of a window _____

6. the width of a TV _____

Tell whether an exact measurement is needed or if an estimate is sufficient. Explain your answer.

7. finding the height and width of a pet carrier

_____

_____

8. finding the width of a bookcase to fit between a chair and the wall

_____

_____

9. finding the height of a tree you will plant in the yard

_____

_____

10. finding the length of a rug to go in a room

_____

_____

Make a list of 3 objects that you think have the given measurements. Check your estimates and record the actual length of each object.

11. 2 feet

12. 3 inches

13. 2 yards

14. $\frac{1}{2}$ inch

_____   _____   _____   _____

_____   _____   _____   _____

Test Prep

15. Which unit of measure gives the most precise measurement of an item?

A foot   C half inch

B inch   D quarter inch

15. What unit of measure would you use to measure the length of a football field?

_____

Use with text pages 148–149.

Customary Units of Length

Complete.

1. 36 in. = _____ ft

2. 4 yd 2 ft = _____ ft

3. _____ ft = 14 yd

4. 4 ft 4 in. = _____ in.

5. _____ ft = 3 mi

6. 215 in. = _____ ft _____ in.

7. 7,200 ft = _____ mi _____ ft

8. 3,550 yd = _____ mi _____ yd

9. 4 mi = _____ yd

Compare. Write >, <, or = for each ◯.

10. 7 yd 1 ft ◯ 25 ft

11. 38 in. ◯ 3 ft

12. 45 ft ◯ 500 in.

13. 7 ft 8 in. ◯ 100 in.

14. 16,000 ft ◯ 3 mi 200 ft

15. 6 ft 6 in. ◯ 75 in.

**Which unit would you use to measure each?
Write _inch, foot, yard,_ or _mile._**

16. the length of a goldfish _____

17. the height of a flagpole _____

18. the width of an elephant's ear _____

19. the distance between two cities _____

Test Prep

20. The bookcase in class 5A is 64 inches long. The bookcase in class 5B is 2 feet shorter. How many inches shorter is the bookcase in class 5B?

    A 2 in.   c 24 in.

    B 12 in.   D 40 in.

21. Juan is 4 feet tall. Marina is 52 inches tall. Who is taller? Explain your answer.

    _____

    _____

Use with text pages 150–151.

Customary Units of Weight and Capacity

Complete.

1. 3 T = _____ lb

2. _____ qt _____ pt = 15 pt

3. _____ lb = 64 oz

4. _____ lb = $9\frac{1}{2}$ T

5. 13,700 lb = _____ T _____ lb

6. 18 qt = _____ gal _____ qt

7. _____ c = 16 pt

8. 32 pt = _____ gal

9. _____ pt = 48 c

Compare. Write >, <, or = for each ○.

10. 5 pt ○ 9 c

11. 3 T 500 lb ○ 7,000 lb

12. 4 lb ○ 64 oz

13. 3 gal 2 qt ○ 15 qt

14. 36 fl oz ○ 4 c 4 fl oz

15. 48 pt ○ 5 gal 3 qt

Which unit would you use to measure each? Write *oz, lb, T, fl oz, c, pt, qt,* or *gal.*

16. A juice carton holds about 32 _____.

17. A box of paper clips weighs about 3 _____.

18. The capacity of a pitcher is 2 _____.

19. A whale weighs about 2 _____.

Test Prep

20. Lizzie made $1\frac{1}{2}$ gallons of punch for a party. If there are 8 people altogether and each person drinks the same amount, how many cups of punch will each person drink?

   A 2 c

   B 3 c

   C 4 c

   D 6 c

21. Zack fills a 3-gallon container with equal amounts of juice and seltzer. How many quarts of juice are there?

   _____

Use with text pages 152–154.

Metric Units of Length

Measure each line segment to the nearest decimeter, centimeter, and millimeter.

1. •————————————————•

   _____

2. •——————•

   _____

3. •————————————————————•

   _____

4. •————————————————————•

   _____

Complete.

5. 50 dm = _____ m

6. 7 m = _____ cm

7. _____ m = 5,000 cm

8. 40 dm = _____ cm

9. _____ m = 8 km

10. 9,000 mm = _____ dm

Compare. Write >, <, or = for each ○.

11. 40 cm ○ 400 mm

12. 4 km ○ 4,000 m

13. 2,300 mm ○ 22 m

For Exercises 14–15, write the metric unit of length that is reasonable.

14. A door is about 1 _____ wide.

15. A dog is about 5 _____ high.

Test Prep

16. Alita has pieces of rope measuring
    7 meters, 690 decimeters, 680 centime-
    ters, and 7,100 millimeters. Which piece
    of rope is the longest?

    A 7 m   **C** 690 dm

    B 680 cm   **D** 7,100 mm

17. 9 m = _____ cm

    A 0.9   **C** 900

    B 90   **D** 9,000

Use with text pages 156–159.

Name _____ Date _____

Metric Units of Mass and Capacity

Complete.

1. 4 L = _____ mL

2. 6 kg = _____ g

3. _____ t = 9,000 kg

4. _____ dL = 6 L

5. _____ mg = 18 g

6. 500 dL = _____ L

Choose the most reasonable measure for each.

7.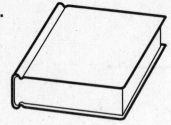

a 950 mg
b 950 g
c 9 kg

8.

a 200 mL
b 2 dL
c 2 L

9.

a 3 kg
b 300 g
c 3,000 mg

Compare. Write >, <, or = for each ○.

10. 6 g ○ 7,000 kg

11. 3 L ○ 3,000 mL

12. 8,200 mL ○ 82 L

13. 38 L ○ 3,800 dL

14. 27 t ○ 27,000 kg

15. 510 g ○ 5,100 mg

For Exercises 16–17, tell which metric unit you would choose to measure each. Explain your choice.

16. the mass of an orange

17. the amount of soup in a cup

_____

_____

 **Test Prep**

18. A car gas tank holds 85 liters of gas. A second car's tank holds 860 deciliters of gas. How much more gas does the second car's tank hold?

A 1 dL

C 10 L

B 10 dL

D 1,000 L

19. If 20 apples have a mass of 3 kg, what is the approximate mass in grams of each apple?

_____

Use with text pages 160–162.

Name _____ Date _____

Add and Subtract Measurements

Add or subtract.

1. 8 ft 4 in.
    − 5 ft 3 in.

2. 18 h 35 min
    + 3 h 18 min

3. 7 T 231 lb
    − 3 T 156 lb

4. 4 lb 12 oz
    + 7 lb 7 oz

5. 8 kg 320 g
    − 2 kg 570 g

6. 52 yd 1 ft
    − 17 yd 2 ft

7. 2 gal 3 qt
    + 1 gal 2 qt

8. 6 m 78 cm
    + 8 m 62 cm

9. 2 gal − 3 pt

10. 42 m 65 cm + 38 cm

11. 4 h 22 min + 42 min

12. 6 m − 12 cm

13. 2 cm 72 mm + 69 mm

14. 15 cm − 58 mm

Algebra • Equations Find the height represented by x.

15. 8 yd − x = 4 yd 2 ft

16. 15 yd − x = 7 yd 2 ft

17. x − 628 m = 903 m

 **Test Prep**

18. Janice cuts a 4-meter piece of wood
    into two pieces. One piece measures
    2 meters 40 centimeters. What is the
    length of the other piece?

    A 1 m 40 cm   c 2 m 60 cm

    B 1 m 60 cm   D 6 m 40 cm

19. Wayne worked for 2 hours and 45
    minutes. Lilly worked for 3 hours and
    15 minutes. How much longer did Lilly
    work than Wayne?

    _____

41   **Use with text pages 164–165.**

Problem Solving Decision: Multistep Problems

Use the table to solve Problems 1–5. Show all your steps.

The Connelly Family Visits the Science Museum			
Museum Tour	Astronomy Show	Dolphin Demonstration	Chemistry Experiment
1:15 P.M.— 2:15 P.M.	1:00 P.M.— 2:00 P.M.	1:30 P.M.— 2:00 P.M.	1:45 P.M.— 2:00 P.M.
2:30 P.M.— 3:30 P.M.	4:00 P.M.— 5:00 P.M.	2:30 P.M.— 3:00 P.M.	2:00 P.M.— 2:15 P.M.

Show Your Work

1. Mr. Connelly wants to go on the museum tour and see the dolphin demonstration. Can he do both? Explain.

   _____

2. Mrs. Connelly wants to see the earlier astronomy show. She also wants to go to the first chemistry experiment. Will this be possible? Explain.

   _____

3. Leila is planning to go to the first museum tour, the second chemistry experiment, and the second astronomy show. Will this be possible? Explain.

   _____

4. Leila's grandmother arrives twenty minutes after the earlier chemistry experiment has started, and she decides to wait and attend a different event. Which events can she attend?

   _____

5. If the family wants to wait for Leila so they can all go to the museum's snack bar, can they go at 4:30 P.M.? Explain.

   _____

Use with text pages 166–167.

Double Bar Graphs

Use the table for Problems 1–5.

Alvin recorded the number of visitors to the wax museum. He recorded the
number of visitors for the busiest months during the years 2001–2002.

Visitors to Wax Museum				
	June	July	August	September
2001	60	152	118	153
2002	140	198	153	147

1. Make a double bar graph in the space
   below.

2. Which month had fewer visitors in 2002
   than in 2001?

   _____

3. How many more people visited the
   museum in 2002 than in 2001?

   _____

4. In 2002, how many more people visited
   the museum in July than in June?

   _____

Test Prep

5. About how many more people visited the
   museum in July, 2002 than in June,
   2001?

   A about 50 people

   B about 100 people

   C about 150 people

   D about 200 people

6. Use the double bar graph above
   showing the number of visitors to
   the wax museum in 2001 and 2002.
   Without ordering numbers, which month
   had the greatest number of visitors for
   2002? Explain how you know.

   _____

   _____

Use with text pages 172–175.

Name _____ Date _____

Histograms

Use the histogram for Problems 1–4.

The histogram shows the amount of money in dollars that people donated to a fund to help save the whales.

Donations

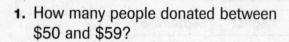

1. How many people donated between $50 and $59?

_____

2. For which interval did the most people donate money to the fund?

_____

_____

3. How many people donated $50 or more to the fund?

_____

_____

4. Looking at the histogram, do you think that people are more likely to donate large or small amounts of money? Explain.

_____

_____

5. Make a histogram for the following information about the years of birth of members of the O'Brien family.

Years of Birth	Number of family members
1960–1969	|
1970–1979	||||
1980–1989	⊬⊬ |
1990–1999	⊬⊬ ||
2000–	||

Test Prep

6. If the histogram above were redone using the intervals 0–19, 20–39, 30–59, and 60–79, which interval would have the most donations?

A 0–19   C 40–59

B 20–39   D 60–79

7. How can a histogram be useful?

_____

_____

_____

                   Use with text pages 176–177.

Name _____ Date _____

Line and Double Line Graphs

Use the graph for Problems 1–7.

The double line graph shows the high and low
temperatures for five consecutive days.

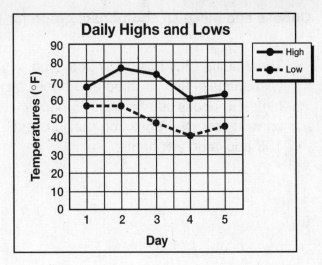

Daily Highs and Lows

1. What were the approximate high and
   low temperatures on Day 2?

   _____

2. Between which two days did the low
   temperature change the least?

   _____

3. Between which two days did the high
   temperature change the most?

   _____

4. On which day was the difference between
   the high and low temperature the greatest?
   the least?

   _____

5. How can you tell on which day the difference between
   the high and low temperatures were either the greatest
   or the least without subtracting the temperatures?

   _____

Test Prep

6. Between which two days was there
   an increase in both the high and low
   temperatures?

   A Day 1–2   c Day 3–4

   B Day 2–3   D Day 4–5

7. How much lower are the high and
   low temperatures on Day 5 than the
   high and low temperatures on Day 1?
   Explain.

   _____

   _____

     Use with text pages 178–180.

Choose an Appropriate Graph

Choose and make an appropriate graph for the data.

Show Your Work

1. The Wildlife Club has many books on wild animals. Rolf counted 250 books on birds, 50 books on snakes, 275 books on wild cats, 150 books on gorillas, and 100 books on elephants.

2. Rolf kept track of the number of books that were checked out of the library each week for 4 weeks.

Books Checked Out	
Week 1	40
Week 2	25
Week 3	55
Week 4	30

Test Prep

3. What graph is the best choice to display the number of sightings of the bald eagle that occurred in each week of July?

   A histogram

   B single-line graph

   C circle graph

   D double-line graph

4. Out of 360 members of the Wildlife Club, 120 preferred lakes, 40 preferred the ocean, 40 preferred deserts, and 160 preferred mountains. Could you use a circle graph to display the data? Explain.

   _____

   _____

Use with text pages 182–183.

Misleading Graphs

The two graphs below show the same information.
Tell which graph seems misleading. Explain your answer.

1.

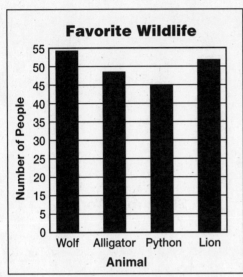

Graph A

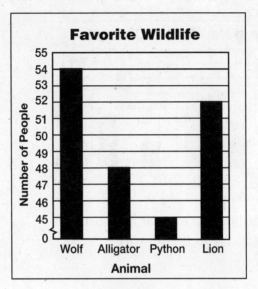

Graph B

2. Explain why the graph displays the data as if Dan hiked almost the same number of miles each day.

3. Make a new line graph, using a scale that more accurately represents the data on the graph.

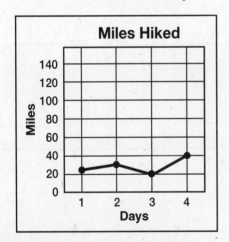

Test Prep

4. In the line graph above, what scale intervals would you use to display the data to show the most difference in the miles that Dan hiked?

   A 20 miles   **c** 5 miles

   B 10 miles   **D** 1 mile

5. How could a graph with missing scale intervals be misleading?

_____

_____

Use with text pages 184–185.

Problem-Solving Decision:
Relevant Information

Use the relevant information in the graph to solve Problems 1–6.

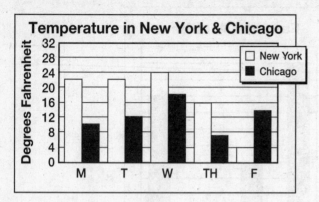

1. What is the difference in temperature between Monday and Friday in New York?

   _____

2. Which city was colder on Tuesday, and by how many degrees?

   _____

3. What is unusual about the temperatures of the two cities on Friday?

   _____

4. How many times does the temperature of New York rise above 20 degrees?

   _____

5. What is the difference between the temperatures in Chicago and New York on Wednesday?

   _____

6. On what day was the difference between the temperatures in the two cities the greatest?

   _____

Show Your Work

Use with text pages 186–187.

Name _____ Date _____

Collect and Organize Data

The table shows the results of a survey of a fifth grade class. Use the table for Problems 1–3.

1. Complete the table.

_____

Favorite Color	Tally Marks	Frequency
Blue	ⵀⵀ I	
Red	ⵀⵀ	
Yellow	III	
Green	II	
Purple	III	
Orange	I	

2. Which color was the most popular? The least popular?

_____

3. What is the difference in frequency between the most popular choice and the least popular choice?

_____

Follow Steps 1–3 on page 192 to survey your classmates about their favorite kinds of books. Then use your results for Problems 4–7.

4. How many students were in your survey?

_____

5. How many categories of books did your survey use?

_____

6. How many students voted for the most popular category? The least popular?

_____

7. Write a short summary of your survey.

_____

 Test Prep

8. Use the table from Problems 1–3. Which two colors were equally popular?

  A Red and Blue

  B Yellow and Green

  C Purple and Orange

  D Yellow and Purple

9. A survey asking people to choose their favorite pet listed the following choices: cat, dog, bird, fish, and hamster. If someone chose cat from the list, can you be sure that a cat is that person's favorite pet? Explain your answer.

_____

     Use with text pages 192–193.

Mean, Median, Mode, and Range

**Make a line plot for each set of data. Then find the mean,
median, mode, and range.**

1. hours worked each week
33, 38, 27, 34, 39, 40, 39,
40, 34, 39, 33, 38, 34

_____

2. number of movies seen
2, 5, 14, 6, 3, 6, 0, 1, 5,
0, 6, 1, 5, 6, 0, 3, 3, 6,
5, 3

_____

Find the mean, median, and mode of each set of data.

3. 16, 20, 25, 22, 30,
29, 12, 16, 20, 30

_____

4. 20, 12, 35, 16, 34, 28,
34, 28, 1, 30, 15

_____

Algebra • Equations Find *n*.

5. 1, 2, 9, 9, 10, 11, *n*
range: 13   mode: 9
median: 9   mean: 8

6. 2, 4, 6, 8, 10, *n*
range: 8   mode: 6
median: 6   mean: 6

7. 4, 6, 14, 15, 17, 29, *n*
range: 25   mode: *n*
median: 14   mean: 13

Test Prep

8. Dave's math grades are 82, 71, 89, 88,
82, and 92. What is his median grade?

A 82   C 84

B 85   D 88

9. Danielle picked the following weights
of apples: 4 lb, 3 lb, 5 lb, 3 lb, 6 lb, and
3 lb. What is the mean weight of the
apples?

_____

Use with text pages 194–196.

Name _____ Date _____

Make and Use a Stem-and-Leaf Plot

Use the stem-and-leaf plot for Problems 1–4.

1. What does 1|4 mean in this stem-and-leaf plot?

   _____

2. How many people are represented in the data?

   _____

3. **Write About It** Identify any clusters and gaps you see. What do these tell you about the data?

   _____

4. Find the mean, median, mode, and range of the data.

   _____

Ages of People at Camp	
Stem	**Leaf**
1	2 2 2 2 2 3 3 3 4 4 4 4
2	2 5 5
3	6
4	
5	3
6	2

6|2 means 62.

Make a stem-and-leaf plot for the data at the right. Then solve Problems 5–7.

5. What was Amy's highest score? Her lowest?

   _____

6. In which group did Amy have the most scores: forties, fifties, sixties, or seventies?

   _____

7. Find the mean, median, mode, and range of the data.

   _____

Amy's Riding Test Scores
55 58 48 60 62 58 70 56
62 65 61 58 54

 **Test Prep**

8. If you made a stem-and-leaf plot for the following data, which stem would have no leaves?

   10, 32, 14, 18, 6, 18, 4

   A 0   C 1

   B 2   D 3

9. What is the difference between the greatest score and the least score?

Science Quiz Scores	
Stem	**Leaf**
2	2 5 5
3	0 5 5
4	3 5 5 5 6

3|0 means 30.

Use with text pages 198–199.

Name _____ Date _____

Problem-Solving Strategy:
Make a Table

Make a table to solve each problem.

Show Your Work

1. You are saving money to take a camping trip with some friends. You saved $10 in January, and you have increased the amount you saved each month by $4. How much money will you have saved by the end of July?

   _____

2. Your cousin, Miguel, wants to come on the trip. You have told him you will need him to add an equal amount each month to your savings between January and April so the two of you will have a total of $104. How much does he need to add each month?

   _____

3. Your friend, Dave, is also coming on the trip. Dave has saved $7 each month since January. Dave's father will add $1 for every $5 that Dave saves. How much money will Dave have by the end of May?

   _____

4. Part of your camping trip will involve 5 days of hiking. The first day you will hike 2 miles. Each day you will add 1 mile to your hike. How many miles will you have hiked after 5 days?

   _____

5. If you were to start with 2 miles of hiking on the first day and double your miles each day, how many miles will you have hiked after 5 days?

   _____

Use with text pages 200–202.

Draw Conclusions and Make Predictions

The line plot shows the number of books donated each day for the library book fair.
Use the line plot for Problems 1–2.

1. Find the mean, median, and mode of the data.

   _____

2. Use the mean, median, and mode to predict the number of books that will be donated on the next day. Explain your answer.

   _____

   _____

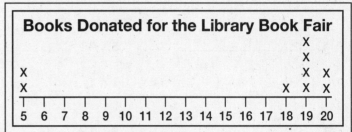

Books Donated for the Library Book Fair

Data Use the stem-and-leaf plot for Problem 3.

3. Find the mean, median, and mode of the data.

   _____

Town Meeting Attendance	
Stem	**Leaf**
0	3 3 3 3
1	5 8 8
2	0 0 0 5
3	2

3|2 means 32.

Test Prep

4. Use the data below. Which most misrepresents the data: the mean, the median, the mode, or the range?

   5 4 14 6 4 4 5

   A mean   **c** median

   B mode   **D** range

5. Use the data from the stem-and-leaf plot above. Which best shows the clusters and gaps in the data: a stem-and-leaf plot or a line plot? Explain your answer.

   _____

53 **Use with text pages 204–206.**

Prime and Composite Numbers

Write all the factors of each number. Then identify the number as *prime* or *composite*.

1. 9 _____

2. 37 _____

3. 21 _____

4. 32 _____

5. 41 _____

6. 36 _____

7. 33 _____

8. 19 _____

9. 11 _____

10. 35 _____

11. 51 _____

12. 15 _____

13. 12 _____

14. 10 _____

15. 50 _____

16. 31 _____

17. 81 _____

18. 100 _____

19. 52 _____

20. 64 _____

21. 99 _____

Test Prep

22. Which number is a composite number?

   A 93   **C** 47

   B 67   **D** 31

23. Is 1 a prime number? Explain your answer.

_____

Use with text pages 224–225.

Prime Factorization

Complete the factor tree. Then write the prime factorization.

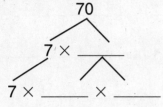

1. 70

7 × ___

7 × ___ × ___

_____

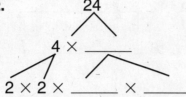

2. 24

4 × ___

2 × 2 × ___ × ___

_____

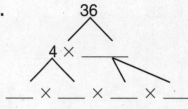

3. 36

4 × ___

___ × ___ × ___ × ___

_____

Write the prime factorization of each number. Use exponents if possible. If the number is prime, write *prime.*

4. 20 _____

5. 21 _____

6. 22 _____

7. 23 _____

8. 24 _____

9. 25 _____

10. 26 _____

11. 27 _____

12. 28 _____

13. 29 _____

14. 30 _____

15. 31 _____

Algebra • Expressions The variable *q* stands for a prime number. Make a factor tree. Then write the prime factorization without exponents for each expression.

16. $12q$

_____

17. $15q^3$

_____

Test Prep

18. The prime factorization of a number is $2^2 \times 3 \times 5 \times 7^2$. What is the number?

A 210   C 1,470

B 420   D 2,940

19. Write the prime factorization of 260. Show how you got your answer.

_____

Use with text pages 226–227.

Greatest Common Factor

List the factors of each number. Then find the greatest common factor of the numbers.

1. 28 _____

32 _____

_____

2. 12 _____

18 _____

_____

3. 21 _____

40 _____

_____

4. 16 _____

32 _____

_____

5. 35 _____

42 _____

_____

6. 20 _____

33 _____

_____

Write the prime factorization using exponents of each number. Then find the greatest common factor (GCF) of the numbers.

7. 12 _____

15 _____

_____

8. 8 _____

18 _____

_____

9. 10 _____

45 _____

_____

10. 60 _____

72 _____

_____

11. 66 _____

99 _____

_____

12. 42 _____

126 _____

_____

Test Prep

13. Find the GCF of 18 and 42.

A 2   **C** 6

B 3   **D** 18

14. Find the GCF of 32 and 36. Explain how you got your answer.

_____

Use with text pages 228–230.

Least Common Multiple

Write the first five multiples of each number.

1. 9 _____

2. 13 _____

3. 20 _____

4. 6 _____

5. 40 _____

6. 21 _____

7. 14 _____

8. 16 _____

9. 22 _____

Write the prime factorization of each number.

10. 14 _____

11. 18 _____

12. 21 _____

13. 24 _____

14. 22 _____

15. 26 _____

16. 28 _____

17. 30 _____

18. 34 _____

Find the LCM of the numbers in each pair. Use either method.

19. 6, 8 _____

20. 4, 7 _____

21. 3, 12 _____

22. 15, 25 _____

23. 6, 7 _____

24. 12, 28 _____

25. 9, 15 _____

26. 24, 36 _____

27. 12, 90 _____

28. 14, 20 _____

29. 30, 40 _____

30. 28, 42 _____

Test Prep

31. Every 12th time Darien goes to the movie theater he gets a free drink. Every 15th time he gets free popcorn. How many times will Darien have to go to get a free drink and free popcorn at the same time?

A 30   C 120

B 60   D 180

32. The downtown bus leaves the station every 15 minutes. The uptown bus leaves the station every 35 minutes. Both buses start the day leaving the station at 7:00 A.M. When is the next time both buses will leave the station at the same time?

_____

Use with text pages 232–234.

Fractions and Mixed Numbers

Study this number line.

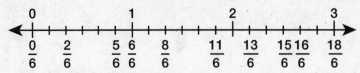

1. Write each missing fraction. Then draw a different model to represent each fraction you wrote.

_____

Write each improper fraction as a mixed number or a whole number.

2. $\frac{11}{6}$ _____   3. $\frac{13}{5}$ _____   4. $\frac{7}{4}$ _____   5. $\frac{12}{6}$ _____   6. $\frac{15}{2}$ _____

Write each mixed number as an improper fraction.

7. $2\frac{1}{3}$ _____   8. $3\frac{4}{5}$ _____   9. $4\frac{2}{3}$ _____   10. $5\frac{1}{6}$ _____   11. $2\frac{4}{5}$ _____

Algebra Expressions Rewrite each expression as a fraction or a division problem.

12. $\frac{x}{y}$ _____   13. $p \div q$ _____   14. $a \div b$ _____   15. $\frac{h}{t}$ _____   16. $\frac{b}{c}$ _____

If j and k are whole numbers not equal to zero, explain how j and k are related in each case. Write $j > k$, $j < k$, or $j = k$.

17. $\frac{j}{k}$ is equal to 1

18. $\frac{j}{k}$ is a fraction between 0 and 1.

19. $\frac{j}{k}$ is a fraction between 1 and 2.

Test Prep

20. Tony needs to frame 7 pictures. He has framed 4 so far. What fraction represents the pictures he has not framed?

   A $\frac{3}{7}$ C $\frac{4}{7}$

   B $\frac{4}{7}$ D $\frac{7}{7}$

21. Lucinda divides 1 quart of juice equally among 3 of her friends. What part of a quart does each friend get?

   _____

Use with text pages 236–238.

Equivalent Fractions and Simplest Form

Complete.

1. $\dfrac{16}{20} = \dfrac{}{5}$

2. $\dfrac{3}{4} = \dfrac{15}{}$

3. $\dfrac{42}{48} = \dfrac{}{8}$

4. $\dfrac{2}{6} = \dfrac{}{18}$

5. $2\dfrac{7}{21} = \dfrac{}{3}$

6. $\dfrac{12}{18} = \dfrac{2}{}$

7. $\dfrac{5}{9} = \dfrac{}{72}$

8. $1\dfrac{8}{12} = \dfrac{}{3}$

Simplify each fraction.

9. $\dfrac{12}{30}$ _____

10. $\dfrac{33}{18}$ _____

11. $\dfrac{28}{8}$ _____

12. $\dfrac{25}{40}$ _____

13. $\dfrac{24}{38}$ _____

14. $\dfrac{28}{12}$ _____

15. $\dfrac{36}{30}$ _____

16. $\dfrac{18}{27}$ _____

17. $\dfrac{24}{44}$ _____

18. $\dfrac{35}{15}$ _____

19. $\dfrac{14}{42}$ _____

20. $\dfrac{48}{12}$ _____

21. $\dfrac{22}{8}$ _____

22. $\dfrac{26}{32}$ _____

23. $\dfrac{36}{24}$ _____

24. $\dfrac{18}{39}$ _____

25. $\dfrac{27}{36}$ _____

26. $\dfrac{42}{48}$ _____

27. $\dfrac{56}{12}$ _____

28. $\dfrac{60}{24}$ _____

Test Prep

29. Simplify $\dfrac{40}{64}$.

A $\dfrac{10}{18}$

C $\dfrac{5}{8}$

B $\dfrac{5}{9}$

D $\dfrac{2}{3}$

30. Marcos spelled 98 of the 100 spelling words correctly. Show the number he spelled correctly as a fraction and write two equivalent fractions for the number.

_____

Use with text pages 240–241.

Problem-Solving Strategy:
Use Logical Reasoning

Use logical reasoning to solve each problem.

Show Your Work

1. The LCM of two numbers is 24. The GCF is 2. The numbers differ by 2. What are the numbers?

   _____

2. The GCF of two numbers is 5. The LCM is 90. The numbers add up to 55. What are the two numbers?

   _____

3. The LCM of two numbers is 72. The GCF is 12. The numbers differ by 12. What are the numbers?

   _____

4. Fraction $\frac{a}{b}$ is equivalent to $\frac{7}{20}$, and $a + b = 135$. Find fraction $\frac{a}{b}$.

   _____

5. Fraction $\frac{c}{d}$ is equivalent to $\frac{9}{13}$, and $d - c = 36$. Find fraction $\frac{c}{d}$.

   _____

6. Explain the method you chose to solve one of the problems above.

   _____

   _____

Use with text pages 242–245.

Name _____   Date _____

Relate Fractions, Mixed Numbers, and Decimals

Write each decimal as a fraction or mixed number in simplest form.

1. 0.7 _____   2. 0.08 _____   3. 0.24 _____   4. 0.6 _____

5. 0.4 _____   6. 3.7 _____   7. 4.25 _____   8. 2.15 _____

Write each fraction or mixed number as a decimal.

9. $\frac{3}{10}$ _____   10. $\frac{1}{2}$ _____   11. $\frac{3}{5}$ _____   12. $\frac{33}{50}$ _____

13. $6\frac{2}{5}$ _____   14. $12\frac{3}{50}$ _____   15. $7\frac{11}{50}$ _____   16. $1\frac{3}{20}$ _____

Use the number line to complete Exercises 17–20.

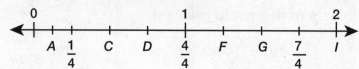

17. Write the decimal represented by point *D*.

_____

18. Write the fraction or mixed number represented by point *G*.

_____

19. Write the mixed number and the decimal represented by point *F*.

_____

20. Which point represents 0.125? Explain.

_____

Test Prep

21. Which fraction is **not** equivalent to $\frac{12}{15}$?

   A $\frac{4}{5}$ C $\frac{24}{30}$

   B $\frac{48}{60}$ D $\frac{36}{40}$

22. Write an equivalent decimal and three equivalent fractions to $\frac{7}{20}$.

_____

       Use with text pages 246–247.

Compare and Order Fractions and Decimals

Compare. Write >, <, or = for each ○.

1. $\frac{5}{7}$ ○ $\frac{3}{5}$ 2. $\frac{3}{7}$ ○ $\frac{5}{8}$ 3. $\frac{12}{14}$ ○ $\frac{6}{7}$ 4. $\frac{7}{8}$ ○ $\frac{5}{6}$

5. $2\frac{7}{15}$ ○ $\frac{36}{15}$ 6. $1\frac{3}{10}$ ○ $1\frac{2}{3}$ 7. $1\frac{5}{12}$ ○ $1\frac{5}{6}$ 8. $3\frac{5}{8}$ ○ $3\frac{1}{2}$

9. $\frac{3}{7}$ ○ 0.4   10. $\frac{3}{5}$ ○ 0.6   11. 0.25 ○ $\frac{1}{3}$ 12. $\frac{3}{8}$ ○ 0.3

13. 1.2 ○ $1\frac{2}{5}$ 14. 5.15 ○ $5\frac{3}{20}$ 15. $2\frac{17}{50}$ ○ 2.35   16. $3\frac{5}{8}$ ○ 3.5

Order each set of numbers from least to greatest.

17. $\frac{1}{6}$, $\frac{2}{9}$, $\frac{7}{36}$ 18. $\frac{23}{50}$, 0.45, $\frac{1}{4}$, $\frac{12}{25}$ 19. $\frac{7}{8}$, $\frac{23}{24}$, $\frac{11}{12}$, 0.75

_____   _____   _____

20. 0.9, $1\frac{7}{12}$, $\frac{3}{4}$, $1\frac{2}{3}$ 21. $2\frac{3}{7}$, $1\frac{6}{7}$, $2\frac{5}{8}$, 2.5   22. 0.75, $\frac{1}{2}$, $\frac{4}{5}$, $\frac{3}{5}$

_____   _____   _____

Algebra • Expressions For each expression, write a value for *n* that will make the expression true.

23. $0.75 = \frac{3}{n}$ 24. $0.7 = \frac{7}{n}$ 25. $\frac{5}{8} < \frac{n}{6}$ 26. $\frac{2}{3} > \frac{n}{9}$

Test Prep

27. Which number is less than $\frac{3}{8}$?

    A $\frac{1}{3}$ C $\frac{1}{2}$

    B 0.4   D $\frac{9}{20}$

28. Peter has three recipes which each call for different amounts of flour. Recipe A calls for $\frac{3}{4}$ cup of flour, recipe B calls for $\frac{2}{3}$ cup of flour, and recipe C calls for $\frac{4}{5}$ cup of flour. Which recipe calls for the most flour? Which calls for the least?

_____

Use with text pages 248–250.

Estimate With Fractions

Estimate the sum or difference. Name the method you used to estimate.

1. $\frac{1}{2} + \frac{3}{8}$ **2.** $\frac{7}{12} + \frac{1}{5}$ **3.** $\frac{1}{6} + \frac{3}{11}$ **4.** $\frac{7}{10} + \frac{8}{9}$

_____   _____   _____   _____

5. $\frac{9}{10} - \frac{1}{6}$ **6.** $\frac{4}{7} + \frac{5}{9}$ **7.** $\frac{7}{8} - \frac{1}{10}$ **8.** $\frac{6}{7} - \frac{5}{12}$

_____   _____   _____   _____

9. $8\frac{1}{5} - 3\frac{3}{4}$ **10.** $65\frac{1}{3} + 21\frac{1}{5}$ **11.** $17\frac{5}{12} - 13\frac{3}{8}$ **12.** $2\frac{4}{9} + 5\frac{1}{10}$

_____   _____   _____   _____

13. $\frac{7}{8} + \frac{5}{11}$ **14.** $96\frac{1}{3} - 35\frac{6}{7}$ **15.** $47 - 37\frac{3}{4}$ **16.** $28\frac{2}{9} + 11\frac{4}{5}$

_____   _____   _____   _____

17. $14 - 3\frac{5}{12}$ **18.** $36\frac{3}{8} - 23\frac{9}{10}$ **19.** $6\frac{2}{3} + 8$ **20.** $50\frac{6}{7} + 22\frac{1}{2}$

_____   _____   _____   _____

21. $3\frac{5}{8} + 6\frac{1}{4} + 2\frac{1}{7} + 2\frac{4}{5}$ **22.** $\frac{1}{4} + 11\frac{10}{11} + 2\frac{1}{2} + \frac{7}{8}$

_____   _____

23. $6\frac{5}{7} + 8\frac{1}{6} + \frac{2}{9} + 12\frac{4}{7}$ **24.** $7\frac{2}{3} + 1\frac{3}{4} + 1\frac{1}{10} + 9\frac{5}{12}$

_____   _____

✓ Test Prep

25. Marcel is $48\frac{3}{8}$ inches tall and his sister Marie is $50\frac{3}{4}$ inches tall. His brother Jacques is $4\frac{1}{2}$ inches taller than Marie. About how much taller than Marcel is Jacques?

    A 2 inches   **C** 7 inches

    B 5 inches   **D** 9 inches

26. Katie is building a bookcase. She decides to buy one piece of wood and cut it into the three lengths she needs, which are $18\frac{7}{8}$ inches, $12\frac{1}{4}$ inches, and $24\frac{3}{4}$ inches. About how long of a piece of wood should Katie buy?

_____

Use with text pages 256–257.

Add With Like Denominators

Add. Write each sum in simplest form.

1. $\dfrac{3}{8} + \dfrac{2}{8}$

2. $1\dfrac{3}{4} + \dfrac{3}{4}$

3. $\dfrac{3}{7} + \dfrac{1}{7}$

4. $4\dfrac{7}{8} + \dfrac{5}{8}$

_____   _____   _____   _____

5. $2\dfrac{1}{5} + 3\dfrac{3}{5}$

6. $\dfrac{5}{11} + \dfrac{5}{11}$

7. $\dfrac{3}{6} + \dfrac{5}{6}$

8. $\dfrac{5}{9} + \dfrac{2}{9}$

_____   _____   _____   _____

9. $7\dfrac{1}{2} + \dfrac{1}{2}$

10. $2\dfrac{3}{4} + 3\dfrac{1}{4}$

11. $5\dfrac{7}{12} + 2\dfrac{11}{12}$

12. $\dfrac{5}{16} + \dfrac{9}{16}$

_____   _____   _____   _____

13. $4\dfrac{4}{7} + 7\dfrac{5}{7}$

14. $1\dfrac{5}{8} + 8\dfrac{1}{8}$

15. $\dfrac{13}{14} + \dfrac{3}{14}$

16. $4\dfrac{3}{10} + 1\dfrac{7}{10}$

_____   _____   _____   _____

17. $\begin{aligned} &\tfrac{2}{5} \\ +\ &\tfrac{1}{5} \end{aligned}$

18. $\begin{aligned} &\tfrac{6}{7} \\ +\ &\tfrac{3}{7} \end{aligned}$

19. $\begin{aligned} 3&\tfrac{4}{9} \\ +\ 6&\tfrac{5}{9} \end{aligned}$

20. $\begin{aligned} 1&\tfrac{7}{10} \\ +\ 2&\tfrac{9}{10} \end{aligned}$

21. $\begin{aligned} 4&\tfrac{5}{6} \\ +\ 2&\tfrac{5}{6} \end{aligned}$

22. $\begin{aligned} &\tfrac{2}{3} \\ +\ 5&\tfrac{1}{3} \end{aligned}$

23. $\begin{aligned} 5&\tfrac{5}{8} \\ +\ 1&\tfrac{1}{8} \end{aligned}$

24. $\begin{aligned} 3&\tfrac{11}{12} \\ +\ &\tfrac{7}{12} \end{aligned}$

Test Prep

25. Mrs. Kojima made a special sauce with $1\dfrac{1}{4}$ cups of soy sauce, $\dfrac{3}{4}$ cup of rice vinegar, and $\dfrac{3}{4}$ cup of sesame oil. How many cups of soy sauce and rice vinegar does she have? Express the answer in simplest form.

   A $1\dfrac{1}{2}$ cups   **C** $2\dfrac{1}{2}$ cups

   B 2 cups   **D** $2\dfrac{3}{4}$ cups

26. Mr. Brown lives $5\dfrac{3}{10}$ miles west of Mr. Kim. Ms. Martinelli lives $3\dfrac{7}{10}$ miles west of Mr. Brown. In simplest form, how far does Ms. Martinelli live from Mr. Kim?

   _____

Use with text pages 258–259.

Add Fractions With Unlike Denominators

Add. Write each sum in simplest form.

1. $\frac{1}{8}$
    $+\frac{1}{3}$

2. $\frac{1}{4}$
    $+\frac{7}{10}$

3. $\frac{7}{12}$
    $+\frac{1}{6}$

4. $\frac{4}{5}$
    $+\frac{2}{3}$

5. $\frac{3}{16}$
    $+\frac{7}{8}$

6. $\frac{1}{6}$
    $+\frac{3}{10}$

7. $\frac{2}{15}$
    $+\frac{3}{5}$

8. $\frac{8}{9}$
    $+\frac{5}{6}$

9. $\frac{1}{2}$
    $+\frac{5}{8}$

10. $\frac{3}{4}$
    $+\frac{3}{8}$

11. $\frac{15}{16}$
    $+\frac{5}{12}$

12. $\frac{6}{7}$
    $+\frac{1}{6}$

13. $\frac{3}{5}$
    $+\frac{11}{12}$

14. $\frac{1}{10}$
    $+\frac{3}{8}$

15. $\frac{9}{11}$
    $+\frac{1}{3}$

16. $\frac{5}{9}$
    $+\frac{2}{5}$

17. $\frac{1}{2} + \frac{5}{6}$

18. $\frac{2}{5} + \frac{1}{10}$

19. $\frac{5}{16} + \frac{7}{12}$

20. $\frac{8}{9} + \frac{1}{18}$

_____

_____

_____

_____

21. $\frac{1}{6} + \frac{1}{12}$

22. $\frac{4}{5} + \frac{3}{4}$

23. $\frac{4}{9} + \frac{2}{3}$

24. $\frac{3}{8} + \frac{3}{4}$

_____

_____

_____

_____

Test Prep

25. On a trip to Boston, Michael's family traveled $\frac{1}{6}$ of the way by train and $\frac{5}{9}$ of the way by bus. They were driven the rest of the way by friends. In simplest form, how much of the trip did they make by train and bus combined?

    A $\frac{23}{27}$

    C $\frac{26}{36}$

    B $\frac{13}{18}$

    D $\frac{31}{54}$

26. Alina picked $\frac{2}{3}$ of a bushel of apples at the orchard, and her little sister picked $\frac{2}{5}$ of a bushel. How much did they pick altogether?

    _____

Use with text pages 260–261.

Add Mixed Numbers With Unlike Denominators

Add. Write each sum in simplest form.

1.
$$2\frac{4}{5}$$
$$+\,4\frac{1}{10}$$

2.
$$1\frac{3}{4}$$
$$+\,1\frac{1}{2}$$

3.
$$5\frac{2}{3}$$
$$+\,5\frac{5}{6}$$

4.
$$9\frac{1}{4}$$
$$+\,7\frac{1}{12}$$

5.
$$2\frac{1}{2}$$
$$3\frac{2}{5}$$
$$+\,2\frac{3}{4}$$

6.
$$4\frac{3}{4}$$
$$3\frac{1}{6}$$
$$+\,4\frac{2}{3}$$

7.
$$1\frac{5}{6}$$
$$2\frac{3}{8}$$
$$+\,1\frac{1}{3}$$

8.
$$10\frac{3}{4}$$
$$13\frac{1}{12}$$
$$+\,11\frac{1}{4}$$

9. $3\frac{5}{8} + 1\frac{1}{2}$

10. $2\frac{2}{3} + 2\frac{2}{9}$

11. $9\frac{3}{10} + 3\frac{2}{5}$

12. $2\frac{3}{16} + 4\frac{7}{8}$

_____ _____ _____ _____

13. $8\frac{5}{8} + 3\frac{2}{3}$

14. $4\frac{1}{5} + 5\frac{2}{3}$

15. $2\frac{9}{10} + 1\frac{5}{12}$

16. $5\frac{4}{5} + 2\frac{1}{4}$

_____ _____ _____ _____

Algebra • Expressions Evaluate. Let $x = \frac{2}{5}$, $y = 2\frac{1}{4}$, and $z = \frac{3}{10}$.

17. $z + x$ **18.** $x + y$ **19.** $z + z$ **20.** $y + z$ **21.** $x + y + x$ **22.** $x + y + z$

_____ _____ _____ _____ _____ _____

Test Prep

23. Molly threw a baseball $42\frac{3}{4}$ feet on her first throw, and then threw her second ball $1\frac{5}{6}$ feet farther than her first. Her third throw was $2\frac{3}{8}$ feet farther than her second, and her fourth throw was $1\frac{11}{12}$ feet farther than her third. How far did she throw her fourth ball?

A $48\frac{7}{8}$ feet   **C** $47\frac{3}{4}$ feet

B $46\frac{1}{2}$ feet   **D** $47\frac{1}{12}$ feet

24. An artist spent $3\frac{1}{2}$ hours painting on Monday, $5\frac{3}{4}$ hours on Tuesday, $2\frac{1}{3}$ hours on Wednesday, and $5\frac{5}{6}$ hours on Thursday. How many hours did she paint in all during those four days?

_____

Use with text pages 262–264.

Subtract With Like Denominators

Subtract. Write each difference in simplest form.

1. $\dfrac{4}{5}$
   $-\dfrac{2}{5}$

2. $\dfrac{9}{10}$
   $-\dfrac{3}{10}$

3. $\dfrac{6}{7}$
   $-\dfrac{5}{7}$

4. $\dfrac{13}{16}$
   $-\dfrac{7}{16}$

5. $3\dfrac{4}{9}$
   $-2\dfrac{2}{9}$

6. 5
   $-2\dfrac{4}{11}$

7. $6\dfrac{1}{4}$
   $-3\dfrac{3}{4}$

8. $\dfrac{5}{6}$
   $-\dfrac{1}{6}$

9. 22
   $-4\dfrac{7}{8}$

10. $7\dfrac{3}{8}$
    $-5\dfrac{7}{8}$

11. $43\dfrac{5}{12}$
    $-27\dfrac{7}{12}$

12. 17
    $-8\dfrac{2}{3}$

13. $12\dfrac{9}{11}$
    $-7\dfrac{3}{11}$

14. $64\dfrac{5}{8}$
    $-38\dfrac{7}{8}$

15. 51
    $-27\dfrac{3}{7}$

16. $38\dfrac{1}{7}$
    $-31\dfrac{3}{7}$

17. $\dfrac{8}{9} - \dfrac{7}{9}$

18. $4 - 2\dfrac{3}{5}$

19. $14\dfrac{1}{3} - 2\dfrac{2}{3}$

20. $35\dfrac{5}{12} - 7\dfrac{11}{12}$

21. $1\dfrac{5}{8} - \dfrac{7}{8}$

22. $25 - \dfrac{5}{6}$

23. $4\dfrac{2}{7} - 3\dfrac{5}{7}$

24. $62 - 58\dfrac{3}{4}$

Test Prep

25. On the first day of a trip from Maine to Washington, Catherine drove $402\dfrac{7}{10}$ miles. On the second day, she drove $35\dfrac{9}{10}$ miles less. How far did she drive on the second day?

   A $365\dfrac{8}{10}$ mi

   B $365\dfrac{1}{10}$ mi

   C $366\dfrac{3}{10}$ mi

   D $366\dfrac{4}{5}$ mi

26. On New Year's Day, Brandon's father was exactly $38\dfrac{7}{12}$ years old and Brandon's brother was exactly $25\dfrac{5}{12}$ years younger than their father. In simplest form, how old was Brandon's brother?

   _____

Use with text pages 266–267.

Subtract With Unlike Denominators

Subtract. Write the difference in simplest form.

1. $\dfrac{3}{4} - \dfrac{2}{3}$ 2. $\dfrac{7}{10} - \dfrac{1}{2}$ 3. $\dfrac{5}{6} - \dfrac{5}{8}$ 4. $\dfrac{1}{3} - \dfrac{1}{4}$

5. $\dfrac{5}{9} - \dfrac{2}{5}$ 6. $\dfrac{11}{12} - \dfrac{1}{8}$ 7. $\dfrac{5}{9} - \dfrac{1}{5}$ 8. $\dfrac{7}{8} - \dfrac{2}{3}$

9. $\dfrac{3}{8} - \dfrac{1}{10}$ 10. $\dfrac{2}{3} - \dfrac{2}{9}$ 11. $\dfrac{1}{3} - \dfrac{5}{16}$ 12. $\dfrac{11}{16} - \dfrac{1}{2}$

13. $\dfrac{4}{5} - \dfrac{1}{6}$ 14. $\dfrac{8}{9} - \dfrac{1}{3}$ 15. $\dfrac{7}{8} - \dfrac{3}{4}$ 16. $\dfrac{5}{8} - \dfrac{1}{12}$

17. $\dfrac{11}{12} - \dfrac{2}{3}$ 18. $\dfrac{9}{10} - \dfrac{4}{5}$ 19. $\dfrac{11}{16} - \dfrac{1}{4}$ 20. $\dfrac{3}{4} - \dfrac{3}{12}$

21. $\dfrac{2}{3} - \dfrac{2}{9}$ 22. $\dfrac{5}{6} - \dfrac{3}{5}$ 23. $\dfrac{1}{6} - \dfrac{1}{8}$ 24. $\dfrac{3}{5} - \dfrac{3}{8}$

Test Prep

25. Mr. O'Toole owned $\frac{1}{2}$ of a bookstore business. He sold $\frac{1}{8}$ of the store to Ms. Chen. How much of the business does Mr. O'Toole own now?

A $\dfrac{3}{8}$ C $\dfrac{2}{3}$

B $\dfrac{1}{2}$ D $\dfrac{3}{4}$

26. Ben started a neighborhood landscaping business. He soon found that about $\frac{3}{5}$ of his time was spent mowing lawns and about $\frac{1}{6}$ of his time was spent raking. How much more of his time was spent on mowing than raking?

Use with text pages 268–269.

Problem-Solving Strategy: Draw a Diagram

Draw a diagram to solve each problem.

Show Your Work

1. At Carver Elementary, there are 355 students altogether. The school has 25 more female students than males. How many males and females does Carver have?

   _____

2. Lara and Maria finished $\frac{3}{4}$ of their homework assignment. Lara did $\frac{1}{4}$ more of the assignment than Maria. What fraction of the assignment did each girl finish?

   _____

3. Five eighths of the students in Mr. Hall's class got an A or a B. Four times as many students got an A than got a B. What fraction of Mr. Hall's class got an A?

   _____

4. Two buildings have 60 floors altogether. Building A has 3 floors for every 2 floors of Building B. How many floors does each building have?

   _____

   _____

5. The grocery store employs 35 cashiers and grocery baggers altogether. There are 5 cashiers for every 2 grocery baggers. How many of each are employed?

   _____

   _____

Use with text pages 270–272.

Subtract Mixed Numbers With Unlike Denominators

Subtract. Write each difference in simplest form.

1. $2\frac{5}{6}$
   $-\ 1\frac{1}{3}$

2. $5\frac{3}{4}$
   $-\ 2\frac{1}{2}$

3. 8
   $-\ 4\frac{3}{10}$

4. $1\frac{1}{3}$
   $-\ 1\frac{1}{4}$

5. $5\frac{3}{4}$
   $-\ 2\frac{2}{3}$

6. $8\ \frac{3}{5}$
   $-\ 3\frac{1}{10}$

7. 2
   $-\ \frac{1}{9}$

8. $6\frac{11}{16}$
   $-\ 4\ \frac{3}{8}$

9. $9\frac{1}{3} - 3\frac{5}{8}$

10. $3\frac{7}{12} - 1\frac{3}{4}$

11. $8\frac{4}{5} - 5\frac{5}{8}$

12. $3 - 1\frac{6}{11}$

13. $9\frac{2}{9} - 7$

14. $12\frac{3}{4} - 8\frac{2}{5}$

15. $10\frac{9}{10} - 5\frac{1}{5}$

16. $4\frac{1}{4} - 2\frac{7}{8}$

Write >, <, or =.

17. $6 - 4\frac{3}{5} \bigcirc 4 - 2\frac{7}{10}$

18. $5\frac{4}{9} - 1\frac{1}{3} \bigcirc 10\frac{2}{3} - 6\frac{1}{9}$

19. $7\frac{3}{4} - 2\frac{1}{2} \bigcirc 9\frac{7}{8} - 4\frac{2}{3}$

20. $1\frac{5}{6} - 1\frac{1}{3} \bigcirc 1\frac{1}{2} - 1\frac{1}{4}$

Mental Math Use mental math to subtract.

21. $6\frac{1}{4} - 2\frac{1}{4}$

22. $5\frac{2}{3} - 4\frac{1}{3}$

23. $10\frac{1}{8} - 7$

24. $6\frac{3}{4} - 1\frac{1}{2}$

Test Prep

25. Elmer made 5 strawberry pies for the Thanksgiving dinner, but couldn't resist them. By Thanksgiving Day, he had eaten $2\frac{5}{12}$ of the pies. How many of the pies did he have left?

    A $3\frac{1}{2}$

    B $3\frac{7}{12}$

    C $2\frac{3}{4}$

    D $2\frac{7}{12}$

26. Emily had two presents to wrap for her mother's birthday, and one piece of wrapping paper that was $3\frac{5}{8}$ feet long. For the first present, she cut off a piece that was $1\frac{2}{3}$ feet long. If she needed at least 2 feet of wrapping paper for the second present, did she have enough for both?

    _____

Use with text pages 274–276.

Name _____ Date _____

Explore Addition and Subtraction With Decimals

Change each decimal to a fraction. Model each addition and subtraction. Write each sum or difference as a decimal.

1. 0.5 + 0.4 _____

2. 0.8 + 0.9 _____

3. 0.6 + 0.6 _____

4. 0.5 − 0.3 _____

5. 0.33 + 0.47 _____

6. 0.65 − 0.17 _____

7. 0.87 − 0.34 _____

8. 0.58 + 0.43 _____

9. 0.55 − 0.23 _____

10. 1.18 + 0.7 _____

11. 0.26 + 1.34 _____

12. 1.69 − 0.8 _____

13. 0.87 − 0.83 _____

14. 0.56 + 0.56 _____

15. 0.47 + 1.03 _____

16. 0.93 + 0.7 _____

17. 2.86 − 0.65 _____

18. 1.23 + 1.62 _____

19. 0.46 + 2.4 _____

20. 2.02 − 0.9 _____

Test Prep

21. Ms. Swenson drove 54.2 miles one day, 6.07 miles the second day, and 28.87 miles the third day. How many miles did she drive on those three days?

   A 88.96   **C** 89.14

   B 89.07   **D** 89.77

22. Of the students at Clemente Elementary School, 0.12 are in the drama program, and 0.2 take art classes. Do more students take art or drama? Use a model to explain.

_____

Use with text pages 282–283.

Add Decimals

Add. Use a calculator to check.

1. 2.36
+ 3.4

2. $12.43
+ 8.76

3. 3.8
+ 87.52

4. 1.987
+ 0.72

5. 264.08
+ 8.713

6. 6.417
+ 8.597

7. 76.03
+ 43.218

8. 49.76
+ 1.899

9. $384.72
+ 24.67

10. 12.8
+ 6.457

11. 0.856
+ 5.7

12. 2.19
+ 43.46

13. $89.60
1.97
+ 46.75

14. 186.44
62.7
+ 0.007

15. 9.876
5.13
+ 3.8

16. 0.5
143.523
+ 97.48

17. 67.943 + 18.03 _____

18. $4.55 + $26.01 + $14.99 _____

19. 0.519 + 0.87 _____

20. 8.47 + 7.211 + 16.408 _____

21. 99.99 + 0.001 _____

22. $422.09 + $67.54 + $77.87 _____

Test Prep

23. Baseball legend Ty Cobb averaged 4.875 home runs per season for his career. Hank Aaron averaged 22.255 more per season than Cobb. How many home runs did Hank Aaron hit per season?

A 27.821   C 26.27

B 27.13   D 26.103

24. In a study of hummingbirds, researchers found that one adult male hummingbird weighed exactly 3.037 grams. An adult female weighed 0.35 grams more. What was the weight of the adult female?

_____

Use with text pages 284–285.

Subtract Decimals

Subtract. Add to check your answer.

1. 6.8
    − 3.9

2. $7.25
    − 4.95

3. 9.4
    − 4.52

4. 28.44
    − 13.71

5. $507.46
    − 74.76

6. 66.531
    − 7.48

7. 0.762
    − 0.075

8. 9.34
    − 4.815

9. 4.72 − 3.88

10. $54.98 − $8.49

11. 0.6 − 0.438

12. 23.56 − 12.072

Add or subtract using mental math.

13. $3.75 + $2.25

14. 0.7 − 0.4

15. 5.63 − 0.21

16. 0.005 + 0.064

17. 6.42 − 1.42

18. 15.63 − 5.12

19. 3.4 + 8.2

20. $6.68 − $2.45

Algebra • Variables   Find the value of x.

21. $5.8 + x = 7.93$

22. $x + \$4.67 = \$9.49$

23. $4.87 - x = 4.3$

24. $x - 14.6 = 2.082$

25. $7.76 - x = 7.53$

26. $\$18.87 + x = \$53.04$

Test Prep

27. Mrs. Patau budgeted $125 per week for groceries for her family. If she spent $53.76 by Tuesday and another $47.28 on Wednesday and Thursday, how much did she have left for the last two days of the week?

    A $19.54   C $23.96

    B $20.86   D $24.06

28. Katrina is running in a marathon that is 26.219 miles. She has run 14.6 miles so far. How much farther does she have to go?

    _____

Use with text pages 286–288.

Estimate Decimal Sums and Differences

Estimate each sum or difference to the nearest tenth.

1. 0.74 + 0.55

2. 0.48 + 0.32

3. 0.78 − 0.63

4. 0.77 − 0.67

5. 0.637 + 0.85

6. 0.518 − 0.371

7. 0.495 − 0.101

8. 0.17 + 0.18

9. 0.83 − 0.464

10. 0.89 + 0.49

11. 0.67 − 0.209

12. 0.704 − 0.658

13. 0.466 − 0.035

14. 0.07 + 0.61

15. 0.15 + 0.084

16. 0.943 − 0.472

17. 0.56 + 0.28 + 0.328

18. 0.808 + 0.49 + 0.163

19. 0.37 + 0.193 + 0.75

Estimate each sum or difference to the nearest whole number.

20. 3.63 + 5.82

21. 16.08 + 9.3

22. 45.927 − 19.83

23. 8.767 − 1.399

24. $97.64 − $43.09

25. 7.79 + 3.011

26. 85.03 − 11.11

27. 70.5 − 54.83

28. 3.991 + 17.6

Test Prep

29. In a scale model of the solar system in which the Sun is 1 yard in diameter, Earth would be 107.457 yards from the sun. Mars would be 199.61 yards from the Sun. To the nearest whole number, estimate how much farther from the Sun Mars is than Earth.

A 90

C 95

B 93

D 97

30. Marcy took second place in her 100-meter freestyle swimming race, with a time of 57.743 seconds. The first-place swimmer won by 3.36 seconds. To the nearest tenth of a second, estimate the winning time.

_____

Use with text pages 290–291.

Problem-Solving Decision:
Choose a Method

Solve. Write the computation method you used.

Show Your Work

1. In Florida, Miami gets 55.91 inches of precipitation per year. Jacksonville gets 51.32 inches of precipitation per year. How many more inches does Miami get?

_____

2. In 2001, Buffalo, New York, got 35.4 inches of snow in one day. Three feet of snow would equal 36 inches. How many inches short of 3 feet of snow was Buffalo?

_____

3. Buffalo had 145.9 inches of snow for 2001. Marquette, Wisconsin, had 72.9 inches more. How many inches of snow fell in Marquette?

_____

4. Honolulu, Hawaii, received 9.14 inches of precipitation for all of 2001. In one day 3.67 inches of rain fell. How many inches of rain fell the rest of the year?

_____

5. In 2001 Boston got 30.72 inches of precipitation. It normally gets 11.81 inches more per year. How many inches of precipitation does Boston get in a year?

_____

Use with text pages 292–293.

Name _____ Date _____

Model Multiplication

Complete the equation represented by each model. Write each answer in simplest form.

1.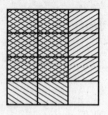

$$\frac{\square}{\square} \times \frac{\square}{\square} = \frac{\square}{\square}$$

2.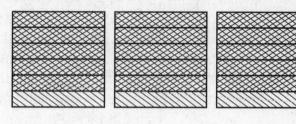

$$\square \times \frac{\square}{\square} = \frac{\square}{\square}$$

3.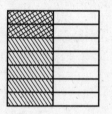

$$\frac{\square}{\square} \times \frac{\square}{\square} = \frac{\square}{\square}$$

4.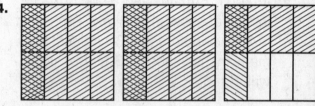

$$\square\frac{\square}{\square} \times \frac{\square}{\square} = \frac{\square}{\square}$$

Use models to find each product. Write each product in simplest form.

5. $\frac{4}{7} \times \frac{1}{3} =$ _____

6. $\frac{2}{5} \times \frac{1}{2} =$ _____

7. $5 \times \frac{2}{3} =$ _____

8. $\frac{3}{5} \times \frac{1}{4} =$ _____

9. $6 \times \frac{1}{3} =$ _____

10. $2 \times \frac{3}{8} =$ _____

11. $\frac{1}{4} \times 2\frac{3}{5} =$ _____

12. $\frac{5}{6} \times 1\frac{1}{3} =$ _____

13. $1\frac{3}{5} \times 1\frac{2}{3} =$ _____

14. $\frac{1}{2} \times 3\frac{2}{5} =$ _____

15. $1\frac{4}{7} \times 1\frac{3}{4} =$ _____

16. $\frac{4}{6} \times 2\frac{5}{6} =$ _____

Test Prep

17. One half of the students in the fifth grade class voted on a class field trip. Two thirds voted to go to the museum. What fraction of the class voted to go to the museum?

_____

18. Tim mixed $\frac{2}{3}$ of $1\frac{3}{4}$ cups of flour with sugar and butter. What fraction of the flour did he use?

A $\frac{1}{6}$

C $\frac{7}{8}$

B $1\frac{1}{2}$

D $1\frac{1}{6}$

Use with text pages 310–313.

Multiply Fractions

Multiply. Write your answer in simplest form.

1. $\frac{1}{5} \times \frac{2}{5}$

2. $\frac{2}{3} \times \frac{1}{4}$

3. $\frac{1}{10} \times 2$

4. $\frac{3}{8} \times \frac{4}{9}$

_____

_____

_____

_____

5. $\frac{1}{3} \times \frac{1}{4}$

6. $\frac{1}{2} \times \frac{6}{12}$

7. $\frac{16}{20} \times \frac{2}{4}$

8. $\frac{4}{7} \times \frac{4}{7}$

_____

_____

_____

_____

9. $6 \times \frac{5}{6}$

10. $\frac{12}{16} \times \frac{1}{8}$

11. $10 \times \frac{3}{5}$

12. $15 \times \frac{2}{3}$

_____

_____

_____

_____

13. $\frac{1}{2} \times \frac{1}{2}$

14. $\frac{1}{5} \times \frac{5}{7}$

15. $\frac{7}{8} \times \frac{8}{9}$

16. $4 \times \frac{3}{12}$

_____

_____

_____

_____

17. $\frac{3}{7} \times \frac{1}{3}$

18. $\frac{1}{10} \times 10$

19. $\frac{2}{3} \times \frac{1}{3}$

20. $\frac{3}{4} \times \frac{1}{6}$

_____

_____

_____

_____

21. $\frac{3}{8} \times \frac{9}{12}$

22. $\frac{2}{9} \times \frac{3}{5}$

23. $\frac{1}{4} \times 8$

24. $\frac{4}{5} \times \frac{3}{4}$

_____

_____

_____

_____

Test Prep

25. On Wednesday, Kelsey had read $\frac{3}{4}$ of a book. On Thursday, she read $\frac{2}{3}$ of the unread pages. What fraction of the book did she still have left to read? Explain how you found your answer.

_____

26. Emily, Brady, Ben, Erin, Ethan, and Jenny each ran an equal part of a two-mile relay race. What part of a mile did each person run?

A $\frac{1}{6}$ C $\frac{2}{3}$

B $\frac{1}{3}$ D $\frac{1}{2}$

Use with text pages 314–315.

Multiply With Mixed Numbers

Multiply. Write each product in simplest form.

1. $1\frac{2}{3} \times \frac{1}{5}$

2. $\frac{4}{7} \times 3\frac{1}{2}$

3. $4 \times 2\frac{3}{8}$

4. $1\frac{5}{6} \times 3$

5. $1\frac{2}{3} \times 2\frac{3}{5}$

6. $2 \times 1\frac{5}{6}$

7. $4\frac{2}{7} \times \frac{1}{8}$

8. $1\frac{1}{3} \times 2\frac{1}{4}$

9. $3\frac{1}{2} \times \frac{3}{5}$

10. $\frac{2}{5} \times 1\frac{3}{4}$

11. $1\frac{1}{3} \times 2\frac{5}{8}$

12. $\frac{4}{5} \times 3\frac{3}{4}$

13. $5 \times 1\frac{3}{4}$

14. $1\frac{1}{6} \times 1\frac{2}{7}$

15. $2\frac{2}{3} \times 2\frac{3}{4}$

16. $2\frac{1}{4} \times 6$

17. $2\frac{2}{5} \times \frac{1}{3}$

18. $4\frac{2}{3} \times 1\frac{3}{7}$

19. $4\frac{3}{8} \times 2\frac{1}{5}$

20. $3\frac{1}{5} \times 2\frac{1}{4}$

Complete each multiplication equation.

21. $\frac{\square}{\square} \times 12 = 9$

22. $\square \times \frac{2}{5} = 4$

23. $\frac{\square}{\square} \times 28 = 8$

24. $\frac{5}{6} \times \square = 15$

Algebra • Functions Complete each function table.

Write each answer in simplest form.

25.

Rule: $y = \frac{2}{3}x$			
x	$3\frac{1}{4}$	$3\frac{2}{3}$	$2\frac{3}{8}$	$2\frac{5}{6}$
y				

26.

Rule: $y = 3\frac{3}{4}x$			
x	$2\frac{4}{5}$	$1\frac{1}{3}$	$3\frac{1}{9}$	$4\frac{4}{5}$
y				

Test Prep

27. Tom bought $2\frac{2}{3}$ pounds of apples. He gave $\frac{3}{4}$ of the $2\frac{2}{3}$ pounds to his friends. How many pounds did he give to his friend?

28. Lonnie worked $2\frac{1}{4}$ hours. Louise worked $\frac{2}{3}$ as long as Lonnie did. How many hours did Louise work?

A $1\frac{5}{12}$ hours   C $1\frac{2}{3}$ hours

B $2\frac{1}{3}$ hours   D $1\frac{1}{2}$ hours

Use with text pages 316–318.

Model Division

Match each question with the correct model. Then complete the division sentence.

1. What is 4 divided by $\frac{1}{3}$?

   $4 \div \frac{1}{3} = \square$

   A

   1   2   3   4

2. What is 4 divided by $\frac{1}{5}$?

   $4 \div \frac{1}{5} = \square$

   B

   1   2   3   4

3. What is 4 divided by $\frac{1}{2}$?

   $4 \div \frac{1}{2} = \square$

   C

   1   2   3   4

Complete each division or multiplication to find *a* and *b*.
Use fraction strips or grid paper for help.

4. $6 \div \frac{1}{3} = a$ $6 \times 3 = b$ _____

5. $7 \div \frac{1}{5} = a$ $7 \times 5 = b$ _____

6. $8 \div \frac{1}{4} = a$ $8 \times 4 = b$ _____

7. $2 \div \frac{1}{6} = a$ $2 \times 6 = b$ _____

Use your answers from Exercises 4–7 to answer Exercises 8–9.

8. What is a unit fraction?

_____

9. What rule can you write about dividing a whole number by a unit fraction?

_____

Divide. Check your answers.

10. $\frac{5}{6} \div \frac{1}{6}$ _____

11. $\frac{4}{5} \div \frac{1}{5}$ _____

12. $\frac{3}{7} \div \frac{1}{7}$ _____

13. $\frac{3}{8} \div \frac{1}{8}$ _____

14. $\frac{2}{7} \div \frac{1}{7}$ _____

15. $\frac{1}{2} \div \frac{1}{2}$ _____

16. $\frac{4}{6} \div \frac{2}{6}$ _____

17. $\frac{6}{9} \div \frac{3}{9}$ _____

18. $\frac{8}{12} \div \frac{4}{12}$ _____

19. $\frac{6}{10} \div \frac{2}{10}$ _____

20. $\frac{4}{5} \div \frac{3}{15}$ _____

21. $\frac{2}{3} \div \frac{3}{9}$ _____

Test Prep

22. Find $\frac{6}{7} \div \frac{1}{7}$. Explain how you found your answer.

_____

23. Beth had 4 feet of rope. She divided each foot into pieces that measured $\frac{1}{4}$ of a foot. How many sections of rope did she then have?

   A $\frac{1}{16}$ **C** 4

   B 8   **D** 16

Use with text pages 320–321.

Divide Fractions

Divide. Write each answer in simplest form.

1. $6 \div \frac{1}{5}$ _____

2. $\frac{1}{8} \div \frac{3}{4}$ _____

3. $\frac{2}{3} \div 6$ _____

4. $15 \div \frac{5}{6}$ _____

5. $\frac{3}{5} \div 3$ _____

6. $\frac{1}{2} \div 8$ _____

7. $10 \div \frac{2}{5}$ _____

8. $3 \div 12$ _____

9. $\frac{3}{4} \div \frac{3}{8}$ _____

10. $\frac{1}{4} \div 12$ _____

11. $4 \div \frac{4}{5}$ _____

12. $\frac{5}{9} \div \frac{3}{9}$ _____

13. $\frac{4}{5} \div \frac{1}{4}$ _____

14. $\frac{1}{4} \div \frac{4}{5}$ _____

15. $\frac{2}{3} \div 2$ _____

16. $2 \div \frac{2}{3}$ _____

17. $\frac{7}{8} \div \frac{3}{4}$ _____

18. $9 \div 4$ _____

19. $4 \div 9$ _____

20. $\frac{5}{8} \div \frac{3}{4}$ _____

21. $\frac{7}{10} \div \frac{3}{5}$ _____

22. $16 \div \frac{1}{2}$ _____

23. $\frac{5}{6} \div \frac{1}{3}$ _____

24. $\frac{2}{9} \div \frac{2}{3}$ _____

25. $\frac{2}{3} \div \frac{5}{9}$ _____

26. $\frac{3}{4} \div \frac{1}{2}$ _____

27. $\frac{5}{12} \div \frac{4}{12}$ _____

28. $\frac{1}{8} \div 9$ _____

Solve.

29. Tammy had 4 pieces of ribbon. She divided each piece by $\frac{1}{5}$. How many pieces did she have then?

30. Tammy has class for $\frac{4}{5}$ of an hour before the break. The class spent $\frac{1}{5}$ of an hour on each of a number of projects. How many projects were they able to work on?

31. After break, the class finished 3 projects in $\frac{3}{4}$ of an hour. They spent the same amount of time on each project. How much time did they spend on each project?

32. Tammy spent $\frac{5}{6}$ of an hour on each of several projects on her own. She spent the same amount of time on each project. She worked for 5 hours. How many projects did she work on?

Test Prep

33. Which is greater, $\frac{4}{5} \div \frac{1}{5}$ or $\frac{1}{5} \div \frac{4}{5}$? Explain your answer.

34. Find $\frac{3}{8} \div \frac{9}{12}$.

   A $\frac{1}{2}$

   C $\frac{1}{3}$

   B $\frac{1}{4}$

   D $\frac{1}{6}$

Use with text pages 322–323.

Divide Mixed Numbers

Rewrite each expression as a multiplication expression.

1. $12 \div 3\frac{1}{4}$

2. $\frac{7}{8} \div 1\frac{2}{5}$

3. $2\frac{2}{5} \div 3$

4. $2\frac{1}{3} \div 1\frac{1}{4}$

_____ _____ _____ _____

Write each quotient in simplest form.

5. $3\frac{1}{3} \div 5$ _____

6. $\frac{3}{4} \div 1\frac{4}{5}$ _____

7. $\frac{5}{8} \div 2\frac{1}{4}$ _____

8. $2\frac{2}{3} \div \frac{2}{3}$ _____

9. $4 \div 1\frac{1}{2}$ _____

10. $5\frac{1}{4} \div \frac{3}{8}$ _____

11. $6 \div 2\frac{1}{4}$ _____

12. $3\frac{6}{7} \div 2\frac{1}{4}$ _____

13. $\frac{3}{4} \div 1\frac{1}{8}$ _____

14. $4 \div 1\frac{3}{5}$ _____

15. $5\frac{1}{3} \div 3\frac{1}{3}$ _____

16. $5\frac{1}{4} \div 3$ _____

17. $6 \div 2\frac{2}{5}$ _____

18. $4\frac{2}{3} \div 2$ _____

19. $2\frac{1}{6} \div 1\frac{1}{3}$ _____

20. $5\frac{1}{2} \div \frac{4}{5}$ _____

21. $\frac{3}{4} \div 2\frac{1}{2}$ _____

22. $1\frac{2}{3} \div 3$ _____

23. $\frac{1}{4} \div 2\frac{2}{3}$ _____

24. $2\frac{2}{3} \div 4$ _____

25. $1\frac{3}{8} \div 4\frac{1}{4}$ _____

26. $3\frac{3}{7} \div 1\frac{1}{3}$ _____

27. $6 \div 1\frac{1}{8}$ _____

28. $\frac{4}{7} \div 2\frac{2}{3}$ _____

Algebra • Expressions Rewrite each expression as a fraction in simplest form. No
    variable equals 0.

29. $3a \div 6$ _____

30. $2 \div 8x$ _____

31. $r \div s$ _____

32. $5p \div 5q$ _____

33. $6m \div \frac{9}{n}$ _____

34. $\frac{2}{x} \div \frac{4}{xy}$ _____

35. $\frac{a}{b} \div \frac{2a}{b}$ _____

36. $3x \div \frac{xy}{4}$ _____

Test Prep

37. Linda measured $8\frac{2}{3}$ yards of cloth. She
    then cut it into 4 equal pieces. What was
    the length of each piece of cloth?

    _____

38. Rolf measured $8\frac{1}{4}$ yards of cloth. He
    then cut it into pieces each measuring
    $2\frac{3}{4}$ yards. Into how many pieces did he
    cut the cloth?

    A 2   **C** 3

    B 4   **D** 5

Use with text pages 324–326.

Problem-Solving Decision: Choose the Operation

Solve.

1. The world record for the men's long jump is $29\frac{3}{8}$ feet. The women's record for the same event is $24\frac{33}{48}$ feet. How many feet longer is the men's record?

   _____

2. The previous world record for the men's long jump was $29\frac{5}{24}$ feet. How long are the two record men's jumps altogether?

   _____

3. Each lap of the Indianapolis 500, a 500 mile car race, constitutes $\frac{1}{200}$ of the race. How many miles are in a lap?

   _____

4. There are 20 nickels in a dollar. Brett has $4 in nickels. How many nickels does he have?

   _____

5. In a survey of favorite team sports, $\frac{1}{8}$ said baseball, $\frac{1}{3}$ said football, $\frac{1}{2}$ said basketball, and the rest said hockey. What fraction said hockey?

   _____

Use with text pages 328–329.

Name _____ Date _____

Explore Multiplication

Use models or fractions to multiply. Write each product as a decimal.

1. 0.2×0.8 _____   **2.** 0.4×0.3 _____   **3.** 0.8×0.8 _____   **4.** 1.2×0.5 _____

5. 0.4×2.6 _____   **6.** 0.7×3.1 _____   **7.** 1.5×0.9 _____   **8.** 0.2×2.8 _____

9. 1.2×0.7 _____   **10.** 0.3×2.4 _____   **11.** 0.8×0.7 _____   **12.** 1.5×0.4 _____

13. 0.1×2.5 _____   **14.** 1.7×0.2 _____   **15.** 0.9×1.1 _____   **16.** 0.9×0.7 _____

17. Which expression below is represented by the hundredths square? _____

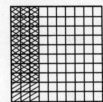

    A 30×80 **C** 0.3×0.8

    B 3×8 **D** $\frac{1}{3} \times \frac{1}{8}$

18. Rewrite the expression below in fractions. Find the product. Write it as a decimal.

    2.1×0.4

_____

Test Prep

19. Sue lives 0.9 km from the school. Kim lives half as far from the school as Sue. How many kilometers does Kim live from the school? Express your answer as a decimal.

_____

20. Find 1.3×0.6.

    A $\frac{78}{10}$ **C** 1.36

    B 0.78 **D** 7.8

83   **Use with text pages 334–335.**

Multiply Whole Numbers and Decimals

Find each product.

1. 4.3×5 _____ **2.** 8×3.7 _____ **3.** 2×8.1 _____ **4.** 5.5×7 _____

5. 12×0.4 _____ **6.** 1.5×8 _____ **7.** 4×0.13 _____ **8.** 1.8×6 _____

9. 4×1.22 _____ **10.** 13.01×8 _____ **11.** 7×23.1 _____ **12.** 4.5×25 _____

13. 120×0.003 ____ **14.** 31×1.8 _____ **15.** 1.6×23 _____ **16.** 20×0.45 ____

17. 4×10.6 _____ **18.** 0.02×78 ____ **19.** 32×0.005 ___ **20.** 2.713×3 ___

21. 18×9.4 _____ **22.** 1.35×6 _____ **23.** 22×0.52 _____ **24.** 30.5×4 _____

25. 12×12.1 _____ **26.** 3×0.267 _____ **27.** 2.015×5 ___ **28.** 42×1.11 ____

Algebra • Expressions Find a value of n to make each statement true.

29. $22 \times n$ is between 80 and 85 _____ **30.** $n \times 85$ is between 175 and 250 _____

31. $142 \times n$ is between 150 and 280 _____ **32.** $n \times 77$ is between 80 and 150 _____

Test Prep

33. Caleb has $45. A jacket originally priced at $65 is now on sale for 0.25 off the original price. Does Caleb have enough money to buy the jacket? Explain your answer.

_____

_____

34. Jackie sold 20 pairs of earrings at the craft fair. Each pair of earrings sold for $15.95. How much money did Jackie receive for all the earrings she sold?

A $3.19   **C** $31.90

B $319   **D** $3,190

Use with text pages 336–337.

Estimate Products

Estimate each product.

1. 36 × 0.42 _____
2. 15 × 28.4 _____
3. 0.401 × 7 _____

4. 7.8 × 33 _____
5. 175 × 0.482 _____
6. 92 × 0.32 _____

7. 2.2 × 61 _____
8. 518 × 0.412 _____
9. 35 × 8.713 _____

10. 0.209 × 19 _____
11. 3 × 0.098 _____
12. 38 × 0.272 _____

13. 11.9 × 43 _____
14. 25 × 3.802 _____
15. 308 × 0.602 _____

16. 0.67 × 51 _____
17. 0.824 × 465 _____
18. 80 × 0.203 _____

19. 2.8 × 181 _____
20. 461 × 0.7 _____
21. 0.319 × 870 _____

22. 62 × 12.5 _____
23. 402 × 1.01 _____
24. 87 × 0.56 _____

25. Rhonda earns $625 a week. She needs to save 0.22 of her weekly check. Estimate how much she needs to save each week. Explain whether the actual amount she needs to save is greater or less than your estimate.

_____

_____

26. Will is buying several books. The cost of the books before tax is $188. The tax is 0.175 of the cost. About how much will his total bill be? Show how you got your answer.

_____

_____

✓ Test Prep

27. Lori works part-time and earns $252 a week. She needs to save 0.275 of her weekly paycheck for her monthly car payment. How should she round the factors to be sure to have enough money? About how much does she need to save each week?

_____

28. Alex gets reimbursed $0.27 for each mile he drives on the job. He drove 421 miles last week. What is a reasonable estimate of the amount he will be reimbursed?

A $12   C $8

B $80   D $120

Use with text pages 338–339.

Multiply Decimals

Multiply.

1. 0.7×0.4 _____   **2.** 0.8×0.2 _____   **3.** 0.5×0.6 _____   **4.** 0.9×0.9 _____

5. 0.21×3 _____   **6.** 0.62×0.5 _____   **7.** 1.8×0.33 _____   **8.** 0.7×3.5 _____

9. 0.79×0.4 _____   **10.** 0.2×0.55 _____   **11.** 0.7×0.94 _____   **12.** 0.2×3.1 _____

13. 15.8×3.6 _____   **14.** 2.04×5.2 _____   **15.** 16.4×1.8 _____   **16.** 1.3×7.82 _____

Algebra • Expressions Choose a value for each variable from the box so that each equation is true.

| 1.04 | 1.4 | 14 | 140 |

17. $n \times 5 = 5.2$ _____   **18.** $0.8 \times n = 11.2$ _____   **19.** $n \times 0.42 = 58.8$ _____

20. $n \times 0.3 = 0.42$ _____   **21.** $m \times n = 19.6$ _____   **22.** $m \times n = 1.456$ _____

Compare. Write >, <, or =.

23. $0.3 \times 0.4 \bigcirc 0.7 \times 0.2$

24. $0.9 \times 0.2 \bigcirc 0.3 \times 0.6$

25. $0.5 \times 0.6 \bigcirc 5 \times 0.06$

26. $0.7 \times 0.4 \bigcirc 1.8 \times 2$

27. $4 \times 0.3 \bigcirc 0.06 \times 2$

28. $0.4 \times 8 \bigcirc 1.6 \times 0.2$

29. $0.4 \times 0.6 \bigcirc 0.8 \times 3$

30. $0.6 \times 0.2 \bigcirc 3 \times 0.04$

Test Prep

31. Use decimals to write a multiplication expression equivalent to 0.6×0.4.

_____

32. Find 1.7×0.3.

A 51   **C** 5.1

B 0.51   **D** 0.051

Use with text pages 340–342.

Name _____ Date _____

Zeros in the Product

Multiply.

1. 0.04
    $\times\ 0.5$

2. 0.002
    $\times\ \ \ 6$

3. 0.14
    $\times\ 0.06$

4. 0.025
    $\times\ \ 0.3$

5. 0.08
    $\times\ 0.09$

6. 0.9
    $\times\ 0.06$

7. 0.42
    $\times\ 0.07$

8. 0.12
    $\times\ 0.09$

9. 0.52
    $\times\ 0.03$

10. 0.77
    $\times\ 0.03$

11. 0.007
    $\times\ \ \ \ 5$

12. 0.085
    $\times\ \ \ \ 4$

13. 0.7
    $\times\ 0.7$

14. 0.16
    $\times\ \ \ 3$

15. 0.17
    $\times\ 0.06$

16. 0.15
    $\times\ \ 0.2$

17. 0.22
    $\times\ 0.07$

18. 0.19
    $\times\ 0.09$

19. 0.26
    $\times\ 0.03$

20. $\ \ \ \ 4$
    $\times\ 0.03$

21. 0.08×0.02 _____

22. 0.7×0.004 _____

23. 5×0.007 _____

24. 0.06×0.06 _____

25. 0.08×0.09 _____

26. 0.04×0.9 _____

27. 0.08×0.25 _____

28. 0.16×0.2 _____

29. 0.15×0.03 _____

Test Prep

30. A cowboy hat costs $42.80 in
    Massachusetts. The sales tax there is
    0.05. With tax, what does the hat cost?

    _____

31. Find 6.1×0.03.

    A 18.3   **C** 0.183

    B 0.83   **D** 0.0183

Use with text pages 344–345.

Problem-Solving Decision: Reasonable Answers

**Solve. Explain why the answer
is reasonable or unreasonable.**

Show Your Work

1. Steve's boss earns $120,000 each year.
   Steve says he earns 0.4 of what the boss
   makes. He earns $30,000 each year. Is
   Steve correct?

   _____

2. Each lap on a track is 0.25 mile. Gillian
   says that if she does 12 laps, she has
   run 3 miles. Is she correct?

   _____

3. A major league baseball team plays 162
   games during the regular season. Karen
   says that a team that wins about 0.6
   of its games will win 60 games. Is she
   correct?

   _____

4. Lisa collects 0.06 interest on her certifi-
   cate of deposit. She says the interest on
   her $10,000 is $600. Is she correct?

   _____

5. Five volunteers from the greyhound
   rescue saved 17 dogs. One of the
   members suggests that they each
   take 3.4 dogs. Is this reasonable?

   _____

Use with text pages 346–347.

Explore Division With Decimals

Model the division and write the quotient in decimal form.

1. 5 ÷ 0.5 _____

2. 4 ÷ 0.2 _____

3. 2 ÷ 0.4 _____

4. 3 ÷ 0.25 _____

5. 4 ÷ 0.8 _____

6. 3 ÷ 0.2 _____

7. 6 ÷ 0.6 _____

8. 5 ÷ 0.25 _____

9. 4 ÷ 0.5 _____

10. 8 ÷ 0.4 _____

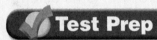 **Test Prep**

11. For each round trip from home to work, Carl uses 0.6 gal of gas. His tank holds 12 gallons. How many round trips can he make on one tank of gas?

_____

12. Karen wants to cut a 4-meter piece of board into pieces each measuring 0.2 meters. How many pieces can she cut from the board?

A 8 **C** 16

B 20 **D** 24

Use with text pages 352–353.

Estimate Quotients

Estimate each quotient.

1. $71 \div 0.28$ _____

2. $221 \div 0.31$ _____

3. $38 \div 0.178$ _____

4. $175 \div 0.23$ _____

5. $12 \div 0.132$ _____

6. $21 \div 0.26$ _____

7. $105 \div 0.601$ _____

8. $893 \div 0.112$ _____

9. $8 \div 0.31$ _____

10. $19 \div 0.199$ _____

11. $47 \div 0.123$ _____

12. $5 \div 0.18$ _____

13. $11 \div 0.24$ _____

14. $7.62 \div 0.475$ _____

15. $25.1 \div 0.261$ _____

16. $3.85 \div 0.28$ _____

17. $63.1 \div 0.21$ _____

18. $9.23 \div 0.194$ _____

19. $62.1 \div 0.122$ _____

20. $18.6 \div 0.261$ _____

21. $288.9 \div 0.28$ _____

22. $49.3 \div 0.483$ _____

23. $88.8 \div 0.185$ _____

24. $48.2 \div 0.281$ _____

25. The fifth grade class is making a quilt. Rusty is cutting a 10-meter piece of cloth into strips each measuring 0.31 meters. About how many strips can he cut from the cloth?

_____

26. The class is spending 2 hours a week on the quilt. They usually work for 0.45 hours each session. About how many sessions are they having each week?

_____

27. Ron is cutting strips of ribbon to go around the border of the quilt. The border is 21.83 meters. Each strip of ribbon measures 0.23 meters. About how many strips will he need for the border?

_____

28. The students raised $41.47 on a bottle drive to help buy cloth for their quilt. For every bottle return, they recieve $0.05. About how many bottles did they return?

_____

Test Prep

29. Estimate the quotient. Explain how you found your answer. $11.58 \div 0.298$

_____

30. Which expression gives the best estimate of $374.2 \div 0.267$?

A $400 \div \frac{1}{4}$

C $300 \div \frac{1}{5}$

B $300 \div \frac{1}{3}$

D $400 \div \frac{1}{8}$

Use with text pages 354–355.

Multiply and Divide by Powers of 10

Multiply or divide by using patterns.

1. $6.02 \div 10^1$ _____

2. $7.21 \div 10^2$ _____

3. 4.82×10^1 _____

4. 5.03×10^2 _____

5. 41.391×10^2 _____

6. $1{,}423.33 \div 10^2$ _____

7. 1.4×10^3 _____

8. $0.726 \div 10^1$ _____

9. $0.23 \div 10^3$ _____

10. 54×10^2 _____

11. 0.6×10^3 _____

12. $4.002 \div 10^1$ _____

13. $735.9 \div 10^2$ _____

14. 72.5×10^3 _____

15. 0.116×10^2 _____

16. $37.82 \div 10^1$ _____

17. $53.09 \div 10^2$ _____

18. 68.14×10^2 _____

19. $1.087 \div 10^3$ _____

20. $5{,}401 \times 10^2$ _____

21. $0.001 \div 10^2$ _____

Algebra • Equations Solve for *a*.

22. $0.4 \div 10^a = 0.04$

23. $72.34 \times 10^a = 7{,}234$

24. $13.9 \times 10^a = 1{,}390$

_____ _____ _____

25. $56.1 \div 10^a = 0.0561$

26. $\dfrac{403}{a} = 4.03$

27. $3.51 \times a = 35.1$

_____ _____ _____

28. $78.02 \div a = 0.07802$

29. $a \times 8.02 = 8{,}020$

30. $\dfrac{2{,}789.3}{a} = 27.893$

_____ _____ _____

Test Prep

31. Explain what you do when you multiply by 10^3 and what you do when you divide by 10^3.

_____

32. Which decimal is equivalent to $0.005 \div 10^2$?

A 5

C 0.5

B 0.0005

D 0.00005

Use with text pages 356–357.

Divide a Decimal by a Whole Number

Divide and check.

1. $3\overline{)6.3}$ _____
2. $6\overline{)1.8}$ _____
3. $8\overline{)20.8}$ _____
4. $6\overline{)31.2}$ _____

5. $38.4 \div 4$ _____
6. $43.5 \div 5$ _____
7. $34.8 \div 6$ _____
8. $77.4 \div 9$ _____

9. $7\overline{)29.4}$ _____
10. $8\overline{)37.6}$ _____
11. $5\overline{)7.15}$ _____
12. $3\overline{)6.33}$ _____

13. $0.95 \div 5$ _____
14. $1.82 \div 7$ _____
15. $4.24 \div 8$ _____
16. $16.72 \div 4$ _____

Algebra • Expressions Evaluate each expression for $p = 1.6$, $q = 3.2$, $r = 8$, and $s = 4$.

17. $\dfrac{p}{s}$ _____
18. $q \div s$ _____
19. $p \div r$ _____
20. $\dfrac{q}{r}$ _____

Algebra • Functions Write the missing values in each table.

21.

Rule: $y = x \div 6$				
x	4.26	0.48	2.28	6.84
y				

22.

Rule: $y = x \div 4$				
x	2.24			3.12
y		0.23	0.12	

Insert a decimal point in each dividend to make each quotient correct.

23. $42 \div 7 = 0.6$

24. $18 \div 3 = 0.06$

25. $301 \div 7 = 4.3$

_____   _____   _____

26. $255 \div 5 = 0.51$

27. $2526 \div 6 = 42.1$

28. $4239 \div 9 = 0.471$

_____   _____   _____

Test Prep

29. Jan has $138.96 for spending money on her trip. She wants to budget the same amount of money for each of the 6 days. How much money can she budget for each day?

_____

30. Which has the greatest quotient?

A $3.78 \div 7$ C $37.8 \div 70$

B $37.8 \div 7$ D $0.378 \div 7$

Use with text pages 358–360.

Write Zeros in the Dividend

Divide. Check using a calculator or estimation.

1. $4\overline{)14}$ _____

2. $2\overline{)3.7}$ _____

3. $5\overline{)8.2}$ _____

4. $15\overline{)0.63}$ _____

5. $32\overline{)16}$ _____

6. $8\overline{)1.4}$ _____

7. $5\overline{)102.3}$ _____

8. $12\overline{)241.5}$ _____

9. $6\overline{)0.9}$ _____

10. $14\overline{)30.87}$ _____

11. $4\overline{)412.2}$ _____

12. $10\overline{)4.3}$ _____

13. $5\overline{)12.1}$ _____

14. $8\overline{)14}$ _____

15. $6\overline{)24.75}$ _____

16. $12\overline{)3}$ _____

17. $4\overline{)28.5}$ _____

18. $5\overline{)6.22}$ _____

19. $2\overline{)9.39}$ _____

20. $16\overline{)2}$ _____

21. $8 \div 25$ _____

22. $11 \div 44$ _____

23. $41.2 \div 8$ _____

24. $8 \div 5$ _____

Compare. Write >, <, or = for each ◯.

25. $4 \div 8 \bigcirc 2.7 \div 6$

26. $14 \div 8 \bigcirc 5 \div 4$

27. $6 \div 8 \bigcirc 4.2 \div 5$

28. $0.6 \div 5 \bigcirc 1.2 \div 10$

29. $0.24 \div 6 \bigcirc 0.6 \div 5$

30. $4 \div 16 \bigcirc 0.75 \div 5$

31. $0.4 \div 8 \bigcirc 0.6 \div 8$

32. $1.1 \div 4 \bigcirc 7 \div 25$

33. $6.2 \div 5 \bigcirc 10 \div 8$

Algebra • Equations Find each missing number.

34. $27 \div n = 4.5$

35. $46 \div n = 5.75$

36. $n \div 6 = 3.45$

37. $n \div 2 = 0.95$

_____ _____ _____ _____

Test Prep

38. Darren had six meters of rope. He cut it into 15 equal pieces. How many meters was each piece?

_____

39. Lois collected money on each of 4 days for a charity. She collected $12.50, $24, $15.50, and $25. What was the average amount of money she collected?

A $1.95

C $2.05

B $20.50

D $19.25

Use with text pages 362–364.

Name _____   Date _____

Repeating Decimals

Change each fraction to decimal form.

1. $\dfrac{1}{3}$ _____

2. $\dfrac{2}{3}$ _____

3. $\dfrac{1}{15}$ _____

4. $\dfrac{2}{15}$ _____

5. $\dfrac{1}{30}$ _____

6. $\dfrac{2}{30}$ _____

7. $\dfrac{3}{30}$ _____

8. $\dfrac{4}{30}$ _____

9. $\dfrac{1}{22}$ _____

10. $\dfrac{2}{22}$ _____

11. $\dfrac{3}{22}$ _____

12. $\dfrac{4}{22}$ _____

13. $\dfrac{1}{18}$ _____

14. $\dfrac{3}{18}$ _____

15. $\dfrac{9}{18}$ _____

16. $\dfrac{7}{3}$ _____

17. $\dfrac{11}{6}$ _____

18. $\dfrac{11}{9}$ _____

19. $\dfrac{11}{5}$ _____

20. $\dfrac{7}{12}$ _____

21. $\dfrac{11}{12}$ _____

22. $\dfrac{8}{3}$ _____

23. $\dfrac{13}{4}$ _____

24. $\dfrac{13}{3}$ _____

25. $\dfrac{22}{6}$ _____

26. $\dfrac{23}{6}$ _____

27. $\dfrac{21}{6}$ _____

28. $\dfrac{13}{6}$ _____

Test Prep

29. **Analyze** Given that $\dfrac{1}{x}$ is a repeating decimal, will $\dfrac{1}{2x}$ be a repeating decimal? Explain and give examples to support your answer.

_____
_____

30. Which of the following best represents the fraction $\dfrac{1}{44}$?

A $0.0\overline{2272}$

C $0.02\overline{272}$

B $0.0\overline{227}$

D $0.022\overline{72}$

Use with text pages 366–367.

Divide a Decimal by a Decimal

Divide. Round to the nearest hundredth. Check that your answer is reasonable.

1. $0.6)\overline{2.4}$ _____

2. $0.5)\overline{0.25}$ _____

3. $1.2)\overline{0.48}$ _____

4. $0.06)\overline{14.3}$ _____

5. $0.4)\overline{17.6}$ _____

6. $0.04)\overline{17.6}$ _____

7. $0.4)\overline{1.76}$ _____

8. $0.04)\overline{0.176}$ _____

9. $0.9)\overline{0.82}$ _____

10. $6.5)\overline{9.1}$ _____

11. $0.25)\overline{0.06}$ _____

12. $0.4)\overline{0.008}$ _____

13. $1.2)\overline{40.8}$ _____

14. $0.03)\overline{6.3}$ _____

15. $0.7)\overline{14.8}$ _____

16. $2.4)\overline{1.8}$ _____

17. $0.05)\overline{72}$ _____

18. $4.5)\overline{245}$ _____

19. $21)\overline{780}$ _____

20. $0.4)\overline{8.34}$ _____

21. Stacy divided 12.8 by 0.04. She found the quotient to be 32. Was she correct? Explain your answer.

_____

_____

22. Without actually dividing, tell which quotient is greater. Explain how you know.

$4.01)\overline{9.03}$ $38.3)\overline{9.03}$

_____

_____

Test Prep

23. Andy spent $10.68 on pens. He paid $0.89 for each pen. How many pens did he buy?

_____

24. Find $12.4 \div 0.42$ to the nearest hundredth.

    A 290.52   C 29.52

    B 2.95   D 3

Use with text pages 368–369.

Problem-Solving Application:
Decide How to Write the Quotient

**Hillside Elementary is taking its chorus to see a musical.
Including teachers, the group consists of 36 people.
Solve and explain how you used each remainder.**

Show Your Work

1. The school hires minivans that can hold up to 8 people. What is the minimum number of minivans the school needs to hire?

   _____

2. The cost of the tickets for the musical is $990. What is the cost for each ticket?

   _____

3. After the musical, the chorus went to Al Covo Italian restaurant. The tables at Al Covo can seat 10 people. How many tables were needed?

   _____

4. On the ride to the city, 54 apples were eaten. Each person ate the same number of apples. How many apples did each person eat?

   _____

5. On the trip back to Hillside, the students discovered that they had collected 49 programs. If each person kept an equal number of programs, how many programs were left for the school?

   _____

Use with text pages 370–372.

Points, Lines, and Rays

Name each figure.

1. ◄●————●————►
   A   B

   _____

2. ●————————●
   P   Q

   _____

3. ●————————►
   R   S

   _____

Describe each pair of lines. Use symbols if possible.

4.
```
   A   B   E
    D     C
```

_____

5.
```
      R
      │
  P ——X—— Q
      │
      S
```

_____

6.
```
  P
  M      Q
         N
```

_____

Draw and label each figure.

7. plane *ABC*

8. $\overrightarrow{UV}$

9. $\overline{AB} \parallel \overline{CD}$

Test Prep

10. For which of the three figures—a line, a line segment, and a ray—can the letters be written in any order?

_____

11. Which of the following describes the figure?

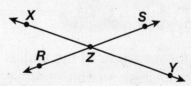

    A *XY* ∥ *RS*   C *XY* and *RS* are rays

    B *XY* ⊥ *RS*   D *XY* and *RS* are intersecting lines

Use with text pages 390–391.

Name _____ Date _____

Measure, Draw, and Classify Angles

In Exercises 1–4, use symbols to name each angle three different ways.

1.

_____

2.

_____

3.

_____

4.

_____

5. Which angle has the greatest measure? The least measure? _____

Classify each angle as *acute*, *obtuse*, *straight*, or *right*.

6.

_____

7.

_____

8.

_____

9.

_____

10.

_____

11.

_____

12.

_____

13.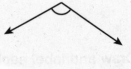

_____

Use a protractor to draw an angle having each measure. Classify each angle as *acute*, *obtuse*, *straight*, or *right*.

14. $35°$ _____ **15.** $145°$ _____ **16.** $110°$ _____ **17.** $75°$ _____

 Test Prep

18. Order the measures of the angles from least to greatest: an obtuse angle, a right angle, a straight angle, and an acute angle.

_____

19. The sum of which two types of angles gives a straight angle?

A acute angle + acute angle

B right angle + right angle

C acute angle + right angle

D obtuse angle + obtuse angle

Use with text pages 392–395.

Triangles

Classify each triangle in two ways.

1.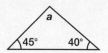
52 yd   48 yd   3 yd

2.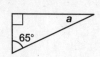
16 cm   22.627 cm   16 cm

3.
8 cm   4 cm   4 cm

4.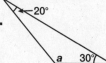
10 m   16 m   18 m

_____   _____   _____   _____

Algebra • Expressions Write an expression to represent *a*. Then find the value of *a*.

5.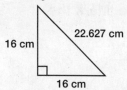
a   45°   40°

6.
65°   a

7.
a   50° 80°

8.
20°   a   30°

_____   _____   _____   _____

9.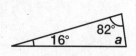
16°   82°   a

10.
60°   a   60°

11.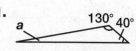
a   130°   40°

12.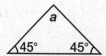
a   45°   45°

_____   _____   _____   _____

Test Prep

13. Is it possible to draw an equilateral
obtuse triangle? Explain your answer.

_____

_____

Use with text pages 396–397.

Congruence

Trace each figure. Use a ruler to measure the sides and a protractor to measure the angles of each figure. Mark the congruent sides and angles.

1.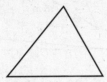

2.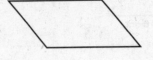

3.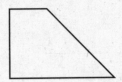

Use the diagram to answer the questions. Explain your reasoning.

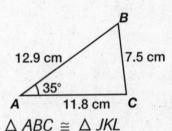

$\triangle ABC \cong \triangle JKL$

4. What is the length of side *KL*? _____

5. What is the measure of ∠*J*? _____

6. What is the length of side *JK*? _____

7. What is the measure of ∠*K*? _____

8. What is the measure of ∠*B*? _____

9. What is the length of side *JL*? _____

10. What is the measure of ∠*C*? _____

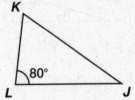

Test Prep

11. The two triangles are congruent. The second triangle has the angles *X*, *Y*, and *Z*. Label it so that △ *DEF* ≅ △ *XYZ*.

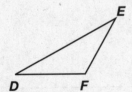 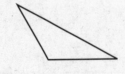

12. △ *ABC* ≅ △ *DEF*. Find the measure of ∠*F*.

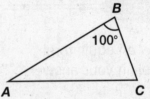 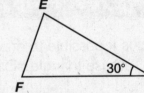

A 30°

B 50°

C 40°

D 100°

Use with text pages 398–399.

Quadrilaterals and Other Polygons

Classify each polygon in as many ways as you can.

1.

_____

2.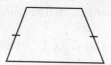

_____

3.

_____

4.

_____

5.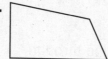

_____

6.

_____

Calculator Write *polygon* or *not a polygon* to classify each figure. If possible, find the measure of each missing angle.

7.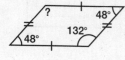

_____

8.

_____

9.

_____

10.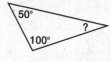

_____

11.

_____

12.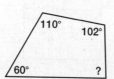

_____

13.

_____

14.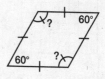

_____

Test Prep

15. **Represent** Draw a quadrilateral that has only two sides parallel. What kind of quadrilateral is it?

_____

16. Find the measure of each of the two missing angles.

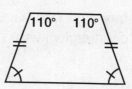

A 60°, 60°   C 70°, 70°

B 120°, 120°   D 140°, 140°

Use with text pages 400–402.

Rotations, Reflections, and Translations

Copy each figure onto grid paper. Then complete the given transformation.

1. Rotate trapezoid *A* 90° clockwise about point *O*. Label the new trapezoid *B*.

2. Translate trapezoid *B* 4 units to the right. Label the new trapezoid *C*.

3. Translate trapezoid *C* 3 units up. Label the new trapezoid *D*.

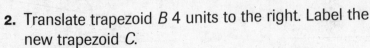

4. Reflect trapezoid *D* across a horizontal line through point *O*. Label the new trapezoid *E*.

5. Which picture(s) show a translation of the shaded figure? _____

A   B   C   D

6. Which picture(s) show a rotation of the shaded figure? _____

A   B   C   D

7. Which picture(s) show a reflection of the shaded figure? _____

A   B   C   D

Test Prep

8. Draw a pentagon on grid paper. Then show a 90° counterclockwise rotation of it.

9. Les reflected <u>right</u> triangle *ABC* about its longest side, *AB*. Which figure best describes the resulting polygon?

  A quadrilateral   **C** rectangle

  B parallelogram   **D** square

Use with text pages 404–406.

Problem-Solving Strategy:
Make a Model

Make a model to solve each problem.

Show Your Work

1. Copy the figure, and then draw it several times. Will this figure tessellate? Explain.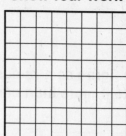

_____

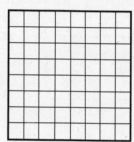

2. Copy the figure, and then draw it several times. Will this figure tessellate? Explain.

_____

3. Copy the figure, and then draw it several times. Explain why this figure will not tessellate.

_____

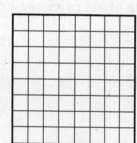

4. What is the shape of the space that is left when you try to tessellate the figures in Problem **3**?

_____

5. Give an example of a figure that will not tessellate. Explain.

_____

_____

103   **Use with text pages 408–410.**

Circles

Use symbols to identify the following parts of this circle.

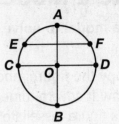

1. radii _____

2. chords _____

3. diameters _____

4. central angles _____

Classify each figure as a *radius, diameter, chord,* or *central angle.* Indicate if more than one term applies.

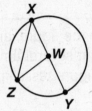

5. $\overline{XY}$ _____

6. $\overline{WZ}$ _____

7. $\overline{XZ}$ _____

8. $\angle ZWY$ _____

9. $\overline{WY}$ _____

10. $\angle XWY$ _____

On a separate sheet of paper, construct a circle that contains all of the following.

11. center *H*

12. diameter *IJ*

13. radius *HK*

14. chord *LM*

15. central angle *KHN*

16. chord *KM*

Test Prep

17. How many chords are drawn in the circle?

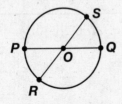

A 2

C 3

B 4

D 5

18. How many new chords can you draw using the given points? What are they?

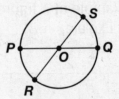

Use with text pages 412–413.

Name _____ Date _____

Symmetry

Trace each figure and turn it. Write *yes* or *no* to tell if it has
rotational symmetry. If it does, tell how many degrees you turned it.

1.

_____

2.

_____

3.

_____

4.

_____

Trace each figure and fold it. Write *yes* or *no* to tell if it has
line symmetry. If it does, write the number of lines of symmetry it has.

5.

_____

6.

_____

7.

_____

8.

_____

9.

_____

10.

_____

Test Prep

11. What kinds of symmetry do an equilateral
and an isosceles triangle have? Give the
degree of rotation and/or the number of
lines of symmetry.

_____

_____

_____

_____

_____

12. How many lines of symmetry does a
square have?

A 1

B 3

C 2

D 4

105   **Use with text pages 414–416.**

Perimeter

Find the perimeter or the missing length.

1.

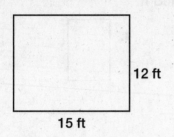

12 ft

15 ft

_____

2.

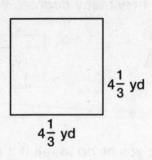

$4\frac{1}{3}$ yd

$4\frac{1}{3}$ yd

_____

3.

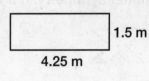

1.5 m

4.25 m

_____

4.

$P = 10$ m

_____

5.

62 ft = P

22 ft

_____

6.

$P = 7\frac{1}{2}$ in.

$1\frac{1}{4}$ in.

_____

Complete the chart below. Each figure in the chart is a rectangle with the given measurements.

	Rectangle	Formula: $P = 2l + 2w$	Perimeter
7.	$l = 5.3$ m, $w = 2.1$ m		
8.	$l = 14$ ft, $w = 7$ ft		
9.	$l = 15$ yd, $w = 4$ yd		

Test Prep

10. Find the length of a side of a square with a perimeter of 30 meters.

A 6.5 m   **C** 7.5 m

B 7 m   **D** 8 m

11. A rectangle has a width of 6 feet and a perimeter of 28 feet. What is its length?

_____

Use with text pages 422–423.

Name _____ Date _____

Problem-Solving Strategy:
Find a Pattern

Use this pattern for Problems 1–3.

Show Your Work

1. Look at the pattern. Draw the figure that comes next.

_____

2. Draw the figure that comes after the figure you drew in Problem 1.

_____

3. Continue the pattern. How many circles will be in the sixth figure?

   _____

_____

Use this pattern for Problems 4–6.

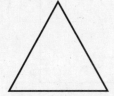 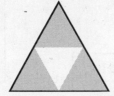 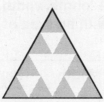

4. Look at the pattern. Draw the figure that comes next.

5. How many shaded triangles are in the figure you drew for Problem 4?

   _____

6. Write the next three numbers that follow the pattern.

   1, 3, 9, 27, . . .

   _____

 Use with text pages 424–426.

Name _____ Date _____

Area of a Parallelogram

Find the area of each figure.

1.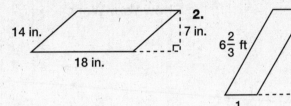

2.

3.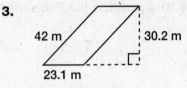

_____ _____ _____

**Figures A and C are rectangles, and figure B is a square.
Use figures A, B, and C for Exercises 4–6.**

4. Find the perimeter of each figure.

_____

5. Find the area of each figure.

_____

6. Suppose that the length and width of each figure are doubled. What is the perimeter and area of each new figure?

_____

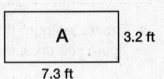

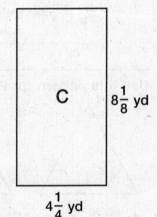

Complete the chart so that it shows the length, width, and perimeter for different rectangles with an area of 24 square meters.

	Area of Rectangle	Length	Width	Perimeter
7.	24 m²	2 m		
8.	24 m²	3 m		
9.	24 m²	4 m		

 **Test Prep**

10. Find the area of a parallelogram that has a base of 14.5 centimeters and a height of 7.2 centimeters.

   A 76.2 cm²   C 98.6 cm²

   B 88.4 cm²   D 104.4 cm²

11. What is the area of the parallelogram?

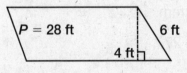

_____

Use with text pages 428–430.

Area of a Triangle

Find the area of each triangle.

1.

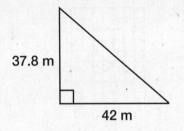

37.8 m

42 m

2.

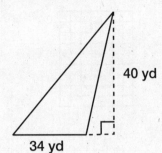

40 yd

34 yd

3.

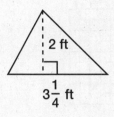

2 ft

$3\frac{1}{4}$ ft

_____ _____ _____

4.

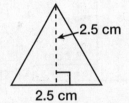

2.5 cm

2.5 cm

5.

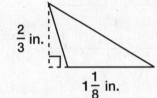

$\frac{2}{3}$ in.

$1\frac{1}{8}$ in.

6.

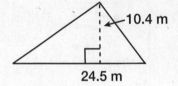

10.4 m

24.5 m

_____ _____ _____

✔ Test Prep

7. A triangle has a height of 4.2 meters and an area of 25.2 square meters. What is the base of the triangle?

  A 6 m   **C** 12 m

  B 8 m   **D** 14 m

8. A triangle has a base of 12 centimeters and an area of 48 square centimeters. What is the height of the triangle?

_____

Use with text pages 432–433.

Perimeter and Area of Irregular Figures

Estimate the perimeter and area of each figure. Each square is 1 cm².

1.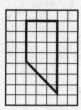

2.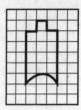

3.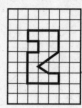

_____   _____   _____

**Find the perimeter and area of each figure.
All intersecting sides meet at right angles.**

4.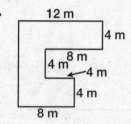

5.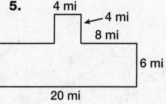

6.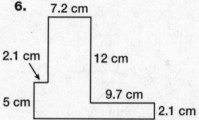

_____   _____   _____

Algebra • Expressions Write an expression to represent the perimeter of each figure.
Then write an expression to represent the area of each figure.

7.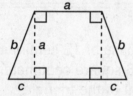

8.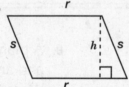

9.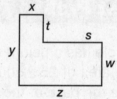

_____   _____   _____

Test Prep

10. Find the area of the figure.

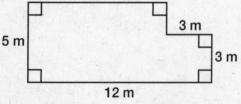

A 54 m²   **C** 72 m²

B 63 m²   **D** 78 m²

11. Find the perimeter and area of the trapezoid.

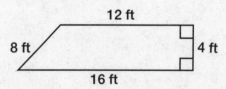

_____

Use with text pages 434–436.

Circumference of a Circle

Find the circumference. Use 3.14 for π. Round your answer to the same degree of precision as given in the diameter or radius.

1.

8.2 m

_____

2.

9 in.

_____

3.

6.45 cm

_____

4. radius = 7 ft

5. diameter = 14 ft

6. radius = 4.138 cm

Express each circumference as a fraction or mixed number in simplest form. Use $\frac{22}{7}$ for π.

7.

$5\frac{1}{4}$ in.

_____

8.

$1\frac{3}{4}$ ft

_____

9.

$4\frac{3}{8}$ ft

_____

10. radius = 21 m

11. diameter = $8\frac{3}{4}$ in.

12. radius = 14 ft

Test Prep

13. Find the circumference of a circle with a diameter of $12\frac{1}{4}$ inches. Use $\frac{22}{7}$ for π.

A $24\frac{1}{4}$ in.   C $38\frac{1}{2}$ in.

B $36\frac{1}{2}$ in.   D $42\frac{1}{4}$ in.

14. Tonya is gluing rectangular pieces of felt around cans to make pencil holders for a craft fair. The cans have a radius of 3.5 centimeters and a height of 10 centimeters. What is the area of each piece of felt? Use $\frac{22}{7}$ for π.

_____

Use with text pages 438–440.

Name _____   Date _____

Solid Figures

Name each solid figure. Then write the number of faces, vertices, and edges.

1.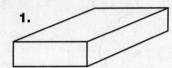

_____

2.

_____

3.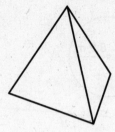

_____

4.

_____

5.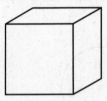

_____

6.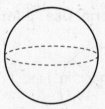

_____

 Test Prep

7. A solid figure has two triangular bases and three rectangular faces. What kind of figure is it?

   A rectangular prism

   B triangular pyramid

   C triangular prism

   D rectangular pyramid

8. Use the table below to predict the number of faces, vertices, and edges a hexagonal pyramid will have. Explain how you found your answer.

   _____

Solid Figure	Faces	Vertices	Edges
Triangular Pyramid	4	4	6
Square Pyramid	5	5	8
Pentagonal Pyramid	6	6	10
Hexagonal Pyramid			

Use with text pages 446–447.

Two-Dimensional Views of Solid Figures

Use cubes to build each figure. On graph paper, draw each figure
from the top, from the side, and from the front.

1.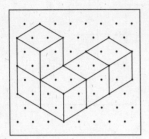

2.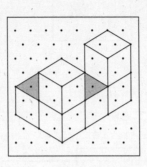

3.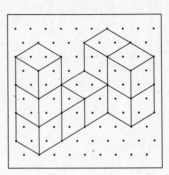

4.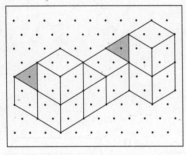

5.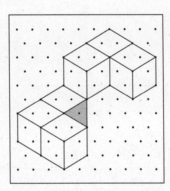

6.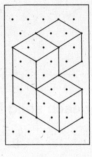

Use cubes to build a three-dimensional figure with these views.
Then draw the figure on triangular dot paper.

7.

   top   side   front

8.

   top   side   front

Test Prep

9. Which solid figure has the least
   number of faces?

   A rectangular prism

   B triangular prism

   C triangular pyramid

   D rectangular pyramid

10. Describe the top view of a cylinder.

   _____

Use with text pages 448–449.

Nets

Predict what shape each net will make.

1.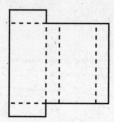

2.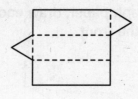

3.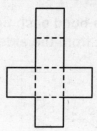

_____   _____   _____

4.

5.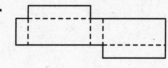

6.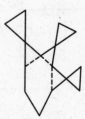

_____   _____   _____

Draw a net for each solid figure.

7.

8.

9.

10.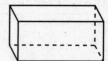

Test Prep

11. A net has four rectangles and two squares. It is most likely a net for which solid figure?

   A rectangular pyramid

   B square pyramid

   C rectangular prism

   D cube

12. A net has three rectangles and two triangles. For what solid figure might it be a net?

   _____

Use with text pages 450–451.

Name _____ Date _____

Surface Area

Determine the surface area of the solid figure. Each square is 1 cm².

1.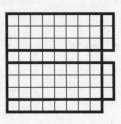

_____

2.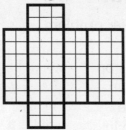

_____

3.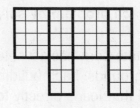

_____

Determine the surface area of each solid figure.

4.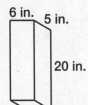

6 in. 5 in.
20 in.

_____

5.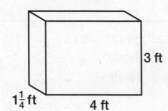

3 ft
$1\frac{1}{4}$ ft   4 ft

_____

6.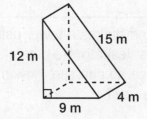

15 m
12 m
9 m   4 m

_____

Copy and complete the table.

	Length of One Side (s) of Cube	Area of One Face (f)	Surface Area of Cube (SA)
7.	4 in.		
8.	6 in.		
9.	8 in.		

Test Prep

10. Karla is covering a box that is 24 centimeters long, 12 centimeters wide, and 8 centimeters high. How many square centimeters of cloth will she need?

A 576 cm²

C 1,152 cm²

B 960 cm²

D 1,624 cm²

11. Find the surface area of the figure.

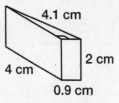

4.1 cm
2 cm
4 cm
0.9 cm

_____

115   **Use with text pages 452–454.**

Problem-Solving Strategy:
Solve a Simpler Problem

Solve each problem by solving a simpler problem.

Show Your Work

1. A state park has 10 nature buildings on its grounds. Each building has its own trail that leads directly to each of the other buildings. How many trails are in the state park?

_____

2. Fred makes a tower using 12 cubes on his desktop. He puts a sticker on every face he can see. How many stickers did he use?

_____

3. Jenna makes a train using the 12 cubes on her desktop. She puts a sticker on every face she can see. How many stickers did she use?

_____

4. Vic's restaurant has square tables that seat one person on each side. For a party, he has to seat 48 people at one long, rectangular table. How many square tables does Vic have to use?

_____

Use with text pages 456–458.

Volume

Determine the volume of each solid figure.

1.

2.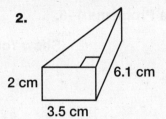
2 cm 6.1 cm
3.5 cm

3.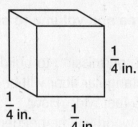
$\frac{1}{4}$ in.
$\frac{1}{4}$ in. $\frac{1}{4}$ in.

4.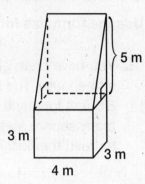
5 m
3 m
3 m
4 m

_____ _____ _____ _____

Copy and complete the chart below.

	Length	Width	Height	Perimeter of base	Area of base	Volume
				Measurements of Rectangular Prisms		
5.	2 ft	4 ft	5 ft			
6.		6 ft	3 ft	26 ft		
7.	10 ft	3 ft	5 ft			
8.	4 ft	7 ft				56 ft³

Choose the most appropriate measure. Write *perimeter*, *area*, or *volume*.

9.	the amount of water in a bathtub	10.	the amount of fencing needed to enclose an outdoor pool
11.	the number of tiles needed to cover the floor of the cafeteria	12.	the number of jellybeans in a jar

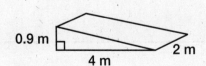 **Test Prep**

13. Find the volume of the solid figure.

0.9 m
4 m
2 m

A 1.8 m³   C 7.2 m³

B 3.6 m³   D 16.2 m³

14. Jeremy plans to cover a wooden box and its lid with 1-in. mosaic tiles. The box is 10 in. long, 6 in. wide, and 3 in. high. How many tiles will Jeremy need?

Use with text pages 460–463.

Problem-Solving Application:
Use Formulas

Use the formulas for area and volume to solve Problems 1–5.

Show Your Work

1. You have been given permission to build a treehouse. The rectangular floor will be 8.5 feet long and 9.5 feet wide. How many square feet of wood will be needed to build the floor?

_____

2. Students are painting a 14-ft by 19-ft mural. If a can of paint covers 75 square feet, what is the least number of cans they need to buy to complete the entire mural?

_____

3. The treehouse will have a roof that is made from plywood. You need a total of 84 square feet of plywood, and the piece you have is 4 feet wide. How long is it?

_____

4. Once the treehouse is built, you are planning to store some boxes of sports equipment in it. The volume of each box is 12 cubic feet. If each box is 6 feet long and 2 feet deep, how wide is it?

_____

5. Give another example of a possible length, width, and depth of a box whose volume is also 12 cubic feet. Explain.

_____

Use with text pages 464–466.

Ratios

Use the stars, circles, squares, and heart below to write each ratio three different ways.

☆☆☆☆☆   ◯◯◯   ▢▢   ♡

1. circles to hearts _____

2. stars to squares _____

3. hearts to stars _____

4. squares to stars _____

5. circles to stars _____

6. hearts to squares _____

7. A rectangle has a length of 14 inches and width of 9 inches. What is the ratio of width to length? _____

8. There are 7 boys and 8 girls in the fifth-grade math club. What is the ratio of girls to boys? _____ ;

9. A rectangular prism has a length of 9 cm, a width of 4 cm, and a height of 5 cm. What is the ratio of length to height? _____

10. Alice asked 25 people what pets they had. She found that 14 people had cats and 11 people had dogs. What is the ratio of dog owners to cat owners?

_____

Test Prep

11. Is the ratio of stars to moons the same as the ratio of moons to stars? Explain your answer and give the ratios of each if different.

_____

12. Find the ratio of rectangles to not rectangles.

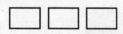

A $\frac{7}{3}$

C 3 to 5

B $\frac{5}{3}$

D 3:7

Use with text pages 484–485.

Name _____   Date _____

Equivalent Ratios

Write four equivalent ratios for each.

1. 3:9 _____

2. $\frac{4}{12}$ _____

3. $\frac{1}{6}$ _____

4. 24 to 12 _____

5. 18:6 _____

6. 2 to 4 _____

Write each ratio in simplest form.

7. 12:18 _____

8. $\frac{24}{32}$ _____

9. 8 to 56 _____

10. 15:45 _____

11. $\frac{16}{24}$ _____

12. $\frac{20}{36}$ _____

13. 27:72 _____

14. 20 to 24 _____

Algebra • Equations **Complete each set of equivalent ratios.**

15. $\frac{2}{7} = \frac{6}{\square}$ _____

16. $\frac{18}{24} = \frac{\square}{8}$ _____

17. $\frac{12}{21} = \frac{\square}{14}$ _____

18. $\frac{10}{15} = \frac{16}{\square}$ _____

19. The ratio of cats to birds in the pet store is 2:9. There are 18 birds in the store. How many cats are in the store?

_____

20. Lucas bought 6 red marbles, 2 blue marbles, and 4 green marbles. Find the ratio of red marbles to all the marbles. Then write it in simplest form.

_____

Test Prep

21. Find all the whole-number ratios that are equivalent to 36:42 and have denominators less than 42.

_____

22. Find the ratio that is equivalent to 18:30.

A $\frac{9}{10}$

C $\frac{24}{40}$

B $\frac{36}{45}$

D $\frac{32}{50}$

Use with text pages 486–487.

Rates

Find the unit rate.

1. $72 in 8 hours

2. 120 miles in 3 hours

3. 75 meters in 5 seconds

_____

_____

_____

4. 180 words in 3 minutes

5. $320 in 4 days

6. 240 km in 6 hours

_____

_____

_____

Complete the unit rate.

7. 900 mi : 15 gal = ☐ mi : 1 gal

8. $5.40 : 12 lb = $☐ : 1 lb

_____

_____

9. 64 h : 16 days = ☐ h : a day

10. 840 km : 12 h = ☐ km : 1 h

_____

_____

Find the distance traveled in the given amount of time.

11. 6 min at 12 m/min _____

12. 0.2 second at 20 ft/s _____

Find the length of time for each trip.

13. 360 mi at 60 mi/h _____

14. 630 ft at 15 ft/s _____

15. 154 m at 22 m/min _____

16. 330 km at 55 km/h _____

Test Prep

17. Casey can buy 6 pens for $5.40 or 8 pens for $6.40. Which is a better buy? Explain your answer.

_____

_____

_____

18. Lin drove for 4 hours at a speed of 60 miles per hour. How far did she drive?

A 240 miles   C 200 miles

B 30 miles   D 15 miles

Use with text pages 488–490.

Proportions

Solve each proportion.

1. $\frac{4}{24} = \frac{x}{6}$ _____

2. $\frac{n}{12} = \frac{3}{4}$ _____

3. $\frac{2}{9} = \frac{k}{18}$ _____

4. $\frac{7}{w} = \frac{28}{32}$ _____

5. $\frac{a}{8} = \frac{15}{20}$ _____

6. $\frac{20}{32} = \frac{30}{f}$ _____

7. $\frac{12}{j} = \frac{14}{21}$ _____

8. $\frac{7}{14} = \frac{b}{10}$ _____

9. $\frac{16}{36} = \frac{m}{72}$ _____

10. $\frac{36}{84} = \frac{15}{z}$ _____

11. $\frac{40}{h} = \frac{20}{36}$ _____

12. $\frac{12}{15} = \frac{q}{50}$ _____

Write the cross products for each pair of ratios.
Do the two ratios form a proportion? Write *yes* or *no*.

13. $\frac{4}{7}$ $\frac{8}{14}$ _____

14. $\frac{2}{3}$ $\frac{6}{9}$ _____

15. $\frac{3}{12}$ $\frac{1}{4}$ _____

16. $\frac{5}{8}$ $\frac{25}{64}$ _____

17. $\frac{9}{24}$ $\frac{3}{6}$ _____

18. $\frac{6}{24}$ $\frac{5}{20}$ _____

19. $\frac{18}{3}$ $\frac{16}{4}$ _____

20. $\frac{9}{27}$ $\frac{5}{15}$ _____

21. $\frac{4}{16}$ $\frac{6}{18}$ _____

22. $\frac{24}{30}$ $\frac{14}{20}$ _____

23. $\frac{15}{25}$ $\frac{12}{20}$ _____

24. $\frac{4}{28}$ $\frac{6}{42}$ _____

25. $\frac{12}{9}$ $\frac{20}{15}$ _____

26. $\frac{8}{6}$ $\frac{12}{9}$ _____

27. $\frac{12}{18}$ $\frac{14}{20}$ _____

Use proportions to complete the chart below.

Muffin Mixings				
28. **Flour**	1 cup	2 cups	3 cups	
29. **Muffins**		24 muffins		60 muffins

Test Prep

30. A study showed that about 1 out of every 50 parts that goes through the assembly line is defective. How many defective parts are likely out of 600 parts? Write the proportion you use to find the answer.

31. Find the missing term in the proportion.
$\frac{12}{27} = \frac{20}{x}$

A 36

B 45

C 42

D 48

Use with text pages 492–494.

Similar Figures and Scale Drawings

Use the scale 1 cm : 5 km to find *n*.

1. 3 cm in the drawing represents *n* km.

_____

2. *n* cm in the drawing represents 25 km.

_____

3. *n* cm in the drawing represents 10 km.

_____

4. *n* cm in the drawing represents 30 km.

_____

A blueprint is made with a scale of $\frac{1}{4}$ in. : 1 ft. Find *n*.

5. *n* in. represents 8 ft _____

6. *n* in. represents 2 ft _____

7. $\frac{1}{2}$ in. represents *n* ft _____

8. $1\frac{1}{2}$ in. represents *n* ft _____

Tell whether the rectangles in each pair are similar. Explain your answers.

9. rectangle A and rectangle B

10. rectangle A and rectangle C

Rectangle	Length	Width
A	9 cm	6 cm
B	12 cm	8 cm
C	28 cm	21 cm
D	15 cm	10 cm

Test Prep

11. The acute angles in these two right triangles are congruent. Are the two triangles similar? Explain how you got your answer.

_____

12. Rectangle *ABCD* is similar to rectangle *WXYZ*. Rectangle *ABCD* has a length of 7 m and a width of 2 m. Rectangle *WXYZ* has a width of 8 m. Find its length.

A 42 m   **C** 36 m

B 32 m   **D** 28 m

Use with text pages 496–498.

Problem-Solving Decision:
Estimate or Exact Answer?

**Solve. Tell whether you used an estimate
or an exact answer, and explain why.**

Show Your Work

1. Tina can buy 3 sweaters for $57 at
   Just Sweaters or she can buy 5 sweaters
   for $102 at Tops Tops. Which is the
   better buy?

   _____

2. A pack of 50 greeting cards cost $2.89
   at the pharmacy, and a pack of 30
   greeting cards cost $1.72 at the stationary
   store. Which is the better buy?

   _____

3. A 32-oz bottle of ketchup costs $1.99
   and a 12-oz bottle of ketchup costs
   $1.19. Which is the better buy?

   _____

4. The Saturday ticket plan gives you
   13 games for $364 per ticket. If you
   buy a full season ticket, you get 81
   games for $2,106 per ticket. Which
   is the better buy?

   _____

5. Al's rent-a-car offers a rate of $48
   each day or a weekly rate of $275.
   If you need the car for 7 days, which is
   the better buy?

   _____

Use with text page 500–501.

Understand Percent

Write the percent of each grid that is shaded.

1.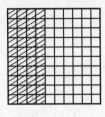

2.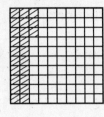

3.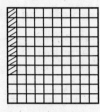

_____

_____

_____

4.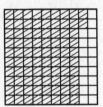

5.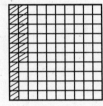

6.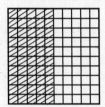

_____

_____

_____

Write each ratio as a percent.

7. $\frac{41}{100}$ _____   8. $\frac{17}{100}$ _____   9. $\frac{3}{100}$ _____   10. $\frac{25}{100}$ _____

11. $\frac{88}{100}$ _____   12. $\frac{99}{100}$ _____   13. $\frac{50}{100}$ _____   14. $\frac{38}{100}$ _____

15. 4 parts out of 100 _____

16. 11 parts out of 100 _____

17. 100 parts out of 100 _____

18. 75 parts out of 100 _____

19. 30 parts out of 100 _____

20. 65 parts out of 100 _____

Write each percent as a ratio in simplest form.

21. 45% _____   22. 8% _____   23. 12% _____   24. 50% _____

25. 43% _____   26. 25% _____   27. 80% _____   28. 20% _____

29. 19% _____   30. 33% _____   31. 98% _____   32. 5% _____

Test Prep

33. A survey showed that 64 out of 100 people voted for road improvements in their town. What percent of the people surveyed voted for road improvements?

34. Find 82% as a ratio in simplest form.

A $\frac{82}{100}$ C $\frac{41}{100}$

B $\frac{41}{50}$ D $\frac{82}{50}$

_____

Use with text pages 506–507.

Relate Fractions, Decimals, and Percents

Copy and complete the table. Write each fraction in simplest form.

	Fraction	Decimal	Percent
1.	_____	0.4	_____
2.	$\frac{7}{10}$	_____	_____
3.	_____	_____	85%
4.	_____	0.18	_____
5.	_____	_____	16%
6.	_____	_____	24%
7.	$\frac{11}{20}$	_____	_____

Algebra • Equations Solve each equation for *n*.

8. $\frac{50}{100} = \frac{1}{n}$ _____

9. $\frac{75}{100} = \frac{n}{4}$ _____

10. $\frac{n}{100} = \frac{9}{20}$ _____

11. $65\% = \frac{13}{n}$ _____

12. $n\% = \frac{3}{5}$ _____

13. $0.17 = n\%$ _____

14. $0.31 = n\%$ _____

15. $\frac{76}{100} = \frac{n}{25}$ _____

16. $\frac{55}{n} = \frac{11}{20}$ _____

17. $48\% = \frac{12}{n}$ _____

18. $22\% = \frac{n}{50}$ _____

19. $n\% = \frac{7}{50}$ _____

20. Jade has a total of 50 photographs for her picture album. She has 24 remaining photographs to place. What percent of all her photographs has she already placed?

_____

21. Al took a survey and found that $\frac{1}{4}$ of the students in his class favored a field trip to a local lake. What percent of the students favored the trip to the lake?

_____

Test Prep

22. The Wild Life Club donates 84% of the money they raise for endangered species. How much out of every $50 they raise do they donate?

_____

23. Express $\frac{3}{20}$ as a percent.

A 23%   **C** 60%

B 30%   **D** 15%

Use with text pages 508–509.

Name _____ Date _____

Compare Fractions, Decimals, and Percents

Which is greatest?

1. $\frac{4}{5}$ 0.78 81% _____

2. $\frac{9}{25}$ 0.35 34% _____

3. $\frac{12}{25}$ 5% 0.49 _____

4. $\frac{2}{5}$ 0.41 38% _____

5. $\frac{3}{8}$ 42% 0.38 _____

6. $\frac{13}{20}$ 7% 0.6 _____

Which is least?

7. $\frac{9}{10}$ 0.8 70% _____

8. $\frac{11}{20}$ 50% 0.3 _____

9. $\frac{3}{5}$ 65% 0.64 _____

10. $\frac{8}{25}$ 5% 0.4 _____

11. $\frac{7}{50}$ 20% 0.1 _____

12. $\frac{21}{25}$ 0.8 82% _____

Order each set from greatest to least.

13. $\frac{1}{4}$ 0.3 40% _____

14. $\frac{2}{3}$ 60% 0.06 _____

15. $\frac{7}{10}$ 72% 0.69 _____

16. $\frac{1}{8}$ 12% 0.2 _____

17. $\frac{19}{20}$ 0.9 80% _____

18. $\frac{14}{25}$ 0.5 60% _____

Algebra • Inequalities Write a number that will make the number sentence true.

19. $\frac{3}{8} < \square < 40\%$

20. $42\% < \square < \frac{1}{2}$

21. $\frac{16}{25} < \square < 66\%$

_____   _____   _____

22. $\frac{3}{5} < \square\% < 0.65$

23. $\frac{8}{25} < \square < 35\%$

24. $0.8 < \square\% < \frac{23}{25}$

_____   _____   _____

Test Prep

25. Each student agreed to collect 50 bottles for the bottle drive. Tim collected 0.6 of the goal. Connie collected 62% of the goal. Leslie collected $\frac{3}{5}$ of the goal. Which student collected the most bottles?

_____

26. Order the set of numbers from least to greatest.

$\frac{7}{25}$ 0.3 20% $\frac{2}{5}$

A 20% $\frac{7}{25}$ 0.3 $\frac{2}{5}$

B $\frac{2}{5}$ $\frac{7}{25}$ 20% 0.3

C $\frac{7}{25}$ 20% 0.3 $\frac{2}{5}$

D 0.3 $\frac{2}{5}$ 20% $\frac{7}{25}$

     Use with text pages 510–512.

Name _____ Date _____

Find 10% of a Number

Find 10% of each number.

1. 56 _____   2. 8 _____   3. 11 _____   4. 2 _____   5. 32 _____

6. 345 _____   7. 5,004 _____   8. 63.2 _____   9. 0.7 _____   10. 1.2 _____

Find 20% of each number.

11. 50 _____   12. 136 _____   13. 28 _____

14. 1,890 _____   15. 4.5 _____   16. 0.5 _____

17. 7.08 _____   18. 432 _____   19. 0.18 _____

Estimate each percent of a number.

20. 19% of 82   21. 8% of 49   22. 13% of 704   23. 22% of 215

_____   _____   _____   _____

Find the number.

24. 10% of a number is 89   25. 10% of a number is 7   26. 20% of a number is 41

_____   _____   _____

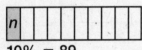
10% = 89

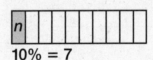
10% = 7

n | | | |
20% = 41

Test Prep

27. Jan says that 10% of 80 is greater than 20% of 40 because 80 is much greater than 40. Is she correct? Explain your answer.

_____

28. 20% of a number is 45. What is the number?

A 90   C 180

B 200   D 225

128   **Use with text pages 514–515.**

Percent of a Number

Solve by writing the percent as a fraction.

1. 70% of 60

2. 40% of 100

3. 25% of 70

4. 15% of 180

_____ _____ _____ _____

5. 60% of 85

6. 55% of 400

7. 20% of 20

8. 50% of 42

_____ _____ _____ _____

Solve by writing the percent as a decimal.

9. 26% of 80

10. 42% of 15

11. 7% of 19

12. 19% of 6

_____ _____ _____ _____

13. 20% of 23

14. 36% of 60

15. 25% of 46

16. 30% of 55

_____ _____ _____ _____

Solve. Use any method.

17. 96% of 100

18. 33% of 50

19. 4% of 111

20. 25% of 16

_____ _____ _____ _____

Algebra • Functions Use the rule to complete each function table.

21. $y = x\%$ of 150

x	y
_____	30
_____	60
_____	90
_____	120

22. $y = 25\%$ of x

x	y
50	_____
60	_____
70	_____
80	_____

23. $y = x\%$ of 150

x	y
5	_____
10	_____
15	_____
20	_____

Test Prep

24. Ruben says his age is 20% of his father's age. His father is 50 years old. How old is Ruben?

A 9

C 11

B 10

D 12

25. Omar's age is 50% less than the age of his 16-year-old brother. In one year, will Omar still be 50% younger than his brother? Explain your answer.

_____

Use with text pages 516–518.

Problem-Solving Application:
Use Circle Graphs

Use the table for Problems 1–5.

What Do You Wear?	
Shoe Style	Number of Students
sneakers	140
hiking boots	30
clogs	20
loafers	10

Show Your Work

1. How many students are represented by 100% in this circle graph?

   _____

2. What percent of the students prefer to wear sneakers?

   _____

3. Write the answer to Problem 3 as a ratio.

   _____

4. Draw a circle graph that shows the data as percents.

   _____

5. Based on the circle graph, what percent of a group of 300 students wear hiking boots? What percent of a group of 400 students wear hiking boots? Explain.

   _____

Use with text pages 520–522.

Make Choices

In each chart, you have one choice from each column. Make an organized list
and a tree diagram to show all the possible choices for each chart.

1.

Sports Events	
Sport	**Level**
Hockey	College
Basketball	Pro
Football	

2.

Drinks	
Size	**Flavor**
Small	Cola
Medium	Orange
Large	Grape
Extra Large	Fruit Punch

3.

Books	
Type	**Level**
Paperback	History
Hardcover	Mystery
	Fantasy
	Romance
	Sci-Fi

_____   _____   _____

You have one choice from each category. Multiply to find the
number of choices possible.

4. 3 cars, 8 colors

5. 4 movies, 4 snacks

6. 6 topics, 3 projects

_____   _____   _____

7. 10 entrees, 7 desserts

8. 4 rings, 5 stones

9. 6 dog, 9 collars

_____   _____   _____

Test Prep

10. Cherie wants to order soup and a sand-
wich. The soups are vegetable, black
bean, and chicken. The sandwiches
are tuna fish, chicken, egg salad, and
tofu burger. How many choices does
she have?

A 4   **C** 12

B 8   **D** 16

11. Angela is writing a story. Each character
will be a boy, a girl, or a talking animal.
Each character will have or will not have
special powers. How many choices does
she have for characters?

_____

Use with text pages 528–529.

Probability Concepts

You turn the cards to the right face down and shuffle.
Then you turn one card face up. Tell which event is
more likely. If possible, describe an event as impossible
or certain.

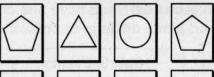

1. circle or trapezoid _____

2. triangle or pentagon _____

3. parallelogram or trapezoid _____

4. triangle or circle _____

5. square or any other shape _____

6. circle or octagon _____

You spin once on the spinner at the right. Tell which event is less
likely. If possible, describe an event as impossible or certain.

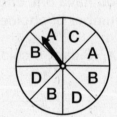

7. C or D _____

8. A or B _____

9. A or E _____

10. C or B _____

11. C or K _____

12. C or A _____

13. B or F _____

14. B or D _____

Test Prep

15. A number cube has numbers 1 to 6.
    What is the probability of tossing a 7?

    A 0

    C $\frac{1}{4}$

    B $\frac{1}{6}$

    D 1

16. Ben and Cassie each have a bag of
    snap cubes. Ben's bag has 3 blue, 3 red,
    4 purple, 2 yellow, and 2 green cubes.
    Cassie's bag has 4 blue, 3 red, 3 purple,
    2 yellow, and 2 green cubes. They take
    turns drawing cubes out of their bags
    until one of them draws a purple cube.
    Whoever draws a purple cube first wins
    the game. Is the game fair? Explain.

Use with text pages 530–531.

Theoretical Probability

You turn the cards to the right face down
and shuffle. Then you turn one card face
up. Express the probability of each event
as a fraction in simplest form.

1. heart _____   2. plus sign _____

3. star _____   4. triangle _____

5. not circle _____   6. not star _____   7. circle or plus sign _____

8. not heart or star _____   9. not triangle or star _____

The chart on the right shows the months in which each of the 24 students in Mrs.
Maxwell's class were born. Each student's name is written on a slip of paper and placed
into a jar. If Mrs. Maxwell picked the name of one student from the jar, what would be the
probability of each event listed below? Express the probability of each event as a fraction
in simplest form.

10. a student born in January–March _____

11. a student born in July–December _____

12. a student born in January–June _____

13. a student born in April–June _____

14. a student not born in April–June _____

15. a student not born in July–September _____

Number of Birthdays in each Month in Mrs. Maxwell's Class	
January–March	6
April–June	8
July–September	3
October–December	7

Test Prep

16. There are 24 marbles in the jar below.
Jason chose one marble from the jar.
What is the probability that it is not gray
or striped?

17. Ashley stood in a center of a ring of
14 children. Eight of the children were
from her school. If she closed her eyes and
spun around, what is the probability that
she faced someone not from her school?

_____

A $\frac{1}{2}$ C $\frac{2}{3}$

B $\frac{7}{12}$ D $\frac{3}{4}$

                       Use with text pages 532–534.

Problem-Solving Strategy: Make an Organized List

Make an organized list to solve each problem.

1. You and 3 of your friends—Gary, Janet, and Simone—are going to the movies. How many different ways can the four of you stand in line for the tickets?

   _____

2. When you get into the theater, Gary and Janet go to buy popcorn and drinks for everyone. Popcorn comes in small, medium, large, and extra-large sizes, and drinks come in small, medium, and large sizes. How many different ways can each person get one popcorn and one drink?

   _____

3. You find out that there are two empty seats in the front row and two seats in the last row. In how many combinations can you and your friends sit? (It does not matter who sits on the left or the right.)

   _____

4. You find four seats together. Gary wants the aisle seat, since he has the longest legs. How many ways can you, Janet, and Simone fill the other seats?

   _____

5. Janet and Simone want to sit together. How many ways are there now for the four of you to be arranged?

   _____

     Use with text pages 536–538.

Experimental Probability

Use index cards to make a set of cards like those to the right. Turn them face down and shuffle. Use the recording sheet to complete each probability experiment. Record each probability as a fraction in simplest form.

O L D
D O G
L O G
F O G

1. Draw a card and get an *O*. Complete 21 draws.

			EXPERIMENT RESULTS		
Event	Theoretical Probability	Prediction ? times in ? trials	Tally of Favorable Outcomes	Number of Favorable Outcomes	Experimental Probability

2. Draw a card and get a *D*. Complete 24 draws.

			EXPERIMENT RESULTS		
Event	Theoretical Probability	Prediction ? times in ? trials	Tally of Favorable Outcomes	Number of Favorable Outcomes	Experimental Probability

3. Draw a card and get a *G*. Complete 12 draws.

			EXPERIMENT RESULTS		
Event	Theoretical Probability	Prediction ? times in ? trials	Tally of Favorable Outcomes	Number of Favorable Outcomes	Experimental Probability

Test Prep

4. Suppose you toss a coin 100 times and record each toss as *heads* or *tails*. How many *heads* would you predict?

   A 100   C 25

   B 50   D 20

5. Repeat Exercise 3 doing 40 draws. How are your results different?

_____

Use with text pages 540–542.

Compound Events

Suppose you roll a number cube labeled 1–6 and spin the spinner once. Find the probability of each compound event.

1. X and 4 _____

2. Z and an even number _____

3. Z and a number less that 5 _____

4. Y and a number greater than 1 _____

5. X or Y and an odd number _____   6. not Z and 3 _____

7. Z and not odd _____   8. X or Z and 1 or 2 _____

Suppose you spin each spinner once. Find the probability of each compound event.

9. heart and 4 _____

10. star and 3 _____

11. plus sign or star, and 2 _____

12. triangle, and 2 or 6 _____

13. circle or star, and even _____   14. plus sign and less than 6 _____

Test Prep

15. There are 8 marbles in a bag. One is red, 1 is blue, 1 is yellow, 1 is purple, 1 is orange, 1 is black, 1 is white, and 1 is green. You select a marble and toss a coin. What is the probability of getting a green marble and tails?

   A $\frac{1}{2}$ C $\frac{1}{8}$

   B $\frac{1}{4}$ D $\frac{1}{16}$

16. The Science Fiction Club decided to choose a president by rolling number cubes labeled 1–6. The first one to roll double fives would be president. What is the probability that Samantha would become president on her first roll?

   _____

     Use with text pages 544–545.

Problem-Solving Application: Make Predictions

Shira played a grab-bag game with her friends. Each person reached into a bag filled with snacks. The table shows the snacks taken by the first 20 of her friends to try the game. Use the table to solve Problems 1–5.

Number of Friends	Snacks Taken
1	a box of mints
4	a box of raisins
5	a bag of peanuts
10	a bag of popcorn

Show Your Work

1. What is the probability of getting no snack? Explain.

   _____

2. What is the probability that friends will get a snack other than raisins?

   _____

3. What is the probability that Shira's friends will get a box of mints?

   _____

4. Suppose Shira invited a total of 40 people to play the grab-bag game. How many people would you expect to get a box of mints out of 40 possible snacks?

   _____

5. If there are 40 friends and 40 snacks, how many more friends would you expect to get popcorn than raisins? Explain.

   _____

Use with text pages 546–548.

Name _____ Date _____

Model Equations

1. In $x - 4 = 5$, what value does x represent?

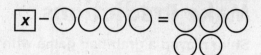

_____

2. Add 3 to both sides of $x - 4 = 5$. What value does x represent?

_____

3. Subtract 2 from both sides of $x - 4 = 5$. What value does x represent?

_____

4. In $3x = 6$, what value does x represent?

_____

5. Multiply both sides of $3x = 6$ by 2. What value does x represent?

_____

6. How can you divide both sides of $3x = 6$ by 3 using fractions?

_____

7. Divide both sides of $3x = 6$ by 3. What value does x represent?

_____

Test Prep

8. Do the equations $x + 4 = 2$ and $x + 9 = 7$ give the same value for x? Explain your answer.

_____

9. Multiply $4x = 12$ by 2. What is the new equation? What is the value of x?

A $2x = 6$; $x = 3$ **C** $8x = 24$; $x = 3$

B $6x = 24$; $x = 4$ **D** $3x = 12$; $x = 4$

Use with text pages 566–567.

Write and Solve Equations

Solve using inverse operations.

1. $z + 24 = 32$ _____

2. $6m = 48$ _____

3. $d - 37 = 23$ _____

4. $k \div 5 = 22$ _____

5. $g - 72 = 15$ _____

6. $f + 267 = 645$ _____

7. $a \cdot 38 = 570$ _____

8. $m + 623 = 814$ _____

9. $b - 184 = 597$ _____

10. $u \div 13 = 12$ _____

11. $180 = q - 34$ _____

12. $81 + n = 278$ _____

13. $64 \cdot z = 1,600$ _____

14. $s \div 56 = 48$ _____

15. $t - 18 = 43$ _____

Use words to describe each equation.

16. $42 + a = 65$ _____

17. $f - 25 = 52$ _____

18. $12 \cdot h = 72$ _____

19. $k \div 56 = 14$ _____

In Problems 20–21, write and solve an equation for each problem.

20. Dan sold 156 tickets in the morning. By the end of the day he had sold 432 tickets. How many tickets did he sell in the afternoon?

21. Alicia gave her friend 6 stamps. She then had 28 left. How many stamps did she have to begin with?

 **Test Prep**

22. Larry had 48 stamps. He divided them evenly onto pages. They covered 6 pages in all. How many stamps did he place on each page? Show the equation you used to solve the problem.

23. Cassie bought 3 tickets to a play. She paid $36 in all. How much did each ticket cost? Choose the equation that describes the situation.

    A $3 \cdot 36 = n$ **C** $36n = 3$

    B $n \div 36 = 3$ **D** $3n = 36$

Use with text pages 568–570.

Problem-Solving Strategy:
Write an Equation

Write an equation to solve each problem.

Show Your Work

1. Some days Tim commutes 4.5 hours to the city. Last month he commuted for 22.5 hours. How many days did he commute to the city?

2. Tim drives $\frac{1}{4}$ as far as Ken does to get to work. If Ken drives 48 miles each way, how far does Tim drive?

3. Tim is now earning $550 per week after receiving an increase of $45 per week. What was Tim's previous weekly salary?

4. Last week Tim worked 42 hours during his five work days. How many hours did he work per day?

5. Ken was hired 2 years after Tim, so he makes 0.8 of what Tim earns. If Tim just received a raise to $600 each week, how much does Ken earn?

6. Tim's and Ken's boss is Anna. She earns $100 more each week than Tim and Ken combined. Using the information from Problem 5, how much does Anna earn each week?

Use with text pages 572–574.

Variables and Functions

Copy and complete each function table.

1. $y = 5x$

x	y
0	
1	
3	
4	

2. $y = x + 8$

x	y
2	
3	
4	
5	

3. $y = 24 \div x$

x	y
2	
4	
6	
8	

4. $y = 12 - x$

x	y
3	
5	
7	
9	

5. $y = 3 + x$

x	y
4	
6	
7	
8	

6. $y = x - 8$

x	y
12	
13	
14	
15	

7. $y = 36 \div x$

x	y
4	
6	
9	
12	

8. $y = 6x$

x	y
4	
5	
6	
7	

9. Use different values of x to complete the function table to the right using the rule $y = x + 2$.

x	y

Test Prep

10. Write four pairs of values that would fit in a function table for the rule $y = 64 \div x$.

_____

11. Choose the pair of values that would fit in a function table for the rule $y = 8x$.

A (8, 1)   **C** (3, 24)

B (2, 8)   **D** (4, 24)

Use with text pages 576–577.

Patterns and Functions

Complete each function table.

1. $y = 3x - 12$

x	y
4	
5	
6	
7	

2. $y = 7 + 4x$

x	y
0	
3	
7	
10	

3. $y = 48 \div 2x$

x	y
1	
4	
	4
	3

4. $y = 17 + 5x$

x	y
0	
	32
5	
	67

Use the function table. Find the value of y for the given value of x.

5. If $x = 8$, $y =$

x	y
0	7
1	8
2	9
3	10

6. If $x = 9$, $y =$

x	y
4	0
5	1
6	2
7	3

7. If $x = 7$, $y =$

x	y
0	3
2	7
4	11
6	15

8. If $x = 5$, $y =$

x	y
0	5
1	9
2	13
3	17

9. What equation describes the relationship between x and y in Problem 7?

_____

10. Write an equation that relates the number of circles (x) to the number of squares (y).

_____

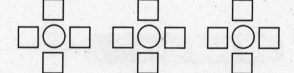

 **Test Prep**

11. Write four pairs of values that would fit in the function table for the rule $y = 7 + 2x$.

_____

12. Use the pairs of values below to find the rule for the function.

(0, 1)   (1, 4)   (2, 7)   (3, 10)

A $2x + 1$ **C** $1 + 4x$

B $3x + 1$ **D** $x + 1$

142   **Use with text pages 578–581.**

Integers and Absolute Value

Write the opposite of each integer.

1. $^-12$

2. $^-34$

3. $^+9$

4. $^-101$

_____

_____

_____

_____

5. $^-5$

6. $^+212$

7. $^+65$

8. $^-3$

_____

_____

_____

_____

9. $^+41$

10. $^-19$

11. $^-39$

12. $^+125$

_____

_____

_____

_____

13. $^-72$

14. $^-94$

15. $^+17$

16. $^+140$

_____

_____

_____

_____

17. $^+81$

18. $^-1$

19. $^-27$

20. $^-58$

_____

_____

_____

_____

Write the absolute value of each integer.

21. $^-3$

22. $^+11$

23. $^-26$

24. $^-11$

_____

_____

_____

_____

25. 0

26. $^-197$

27. $^+7$

28. $^-49$

_____

_____

_____

_____

29. $^-13$

30. $^+1$

31. $^+77$

32. $^+110$

_____

_____

_____

_____

Test Prep

33. Water freezes at 0° C and boils at $^+100°$ C. What other temperature would have the same absolute value as the boiling point, and therefore be the same distance from the freezing point?

   A $^+200°$ C   **c** $^-100°$ C

   B 0° C   **D** $^-200°$ C

34. On a certain math test, the average grade for one class was 84. Students A and C got the same score as each other, but not the same as students B and D. The scores of all four students were the same distance from the average. If students A and C scored 95, what grade did students B and D score?

_____

Use with text pages 586–587.

Compare and Order Integers

Compare. Draw a number line from ⁻10 to ⁺10 and label each integer. Write >, <, or = for each ◯.

1. ⁺7 ◯ ⁻6
2. ⁻2 ◯ ⁻4
3. ⁺4 ◯ 0
4. ⁺1 ◯ ⁻1

5. ⁻5 ◯ ⁺10
6. 0 ◯ 0
7. ⁺6 ◯ ⁻3
8. ⁻5 ◯ ⁺1

9. ⁻5 ◯ ⁺2
10. ⁻1 ◯ ⁻9
11. 0 ◯ ⁻5
12. ⁺5 ◯ ⁻2

13. ⁻5 ◯ ⁻2
14. ⁻4 ◯ 0
15. ⁻3 ◯ ⁺4
16. ⁺1 ◯ ⁻7

Write the integers in order from least to greatest. Draw a number line if you wish.

17. ⁻6, ⁻2, ⁻3, 0
18. ⁺2, ⁺8, ⁻1, ⁻5
19. ⁻7, ⁺2, ⁺1, ⁻1
20. ⁻3, ⁺4, ⁻9, ⁻10

_____ _____ _____ _____

21. ⁻4, 0, ⁺6, ⁻6
22. ⁺1, ⁺2, ⁻3, ⁻4
23. ⁺10, ⁻5, ⁻6, ⁻7
24. ⁻4, ⁻6, ⁺5, ⁻3

_____ _____ _____ _____

25. ⁻7, ⁺8, ⁻8, ⁺6
26. 0, ⁺2, ⁻2, ⁻1
27. ⁻5, ⁺2, ⁺6, ⁻3
28. ⁻4, ⁻9, ⁻1, ⁻6

_____ _____ _____ _____

Test Prep

29. On the same day in January, the temperature in Bangor, Maine was ⁺14°; in Barrow, Alaska it was ⁻29°; in Sapporo, Japan it was ⁺4°; and in Moscow, Russia it was ⁻14°. Which of the following shows the correct order of cities, from coldest to warmest, on that day?

A Sapporo, Moscow, Bangor, Barrow

B Moscow, Barrow, Bangor, Sapporo

C Bangor, Sapporo, Barrow, Moscow

D Barrow, Moscow, Sapporo, Bangor

30. The average surface temperature of Earth's moon is about ⁻130°C. Pluto is about ⁻240°C. In comparison, Jupiter's moon, Io, averages about ⁻143°C and another of its moons, Europa, averages about ⁻173°C. Which of these bodies has the greatest average temperature?

_____

Use with text pages 588–590.

Model Addition of Integers

Use two-color counters to find each sum.

1. $^-4 + {}^+3$

2. $^-3 + {}^-3$

3. $^+4 + {}^+1$

4. $^-10 + {}^+2$

_____

_____

_____

_____

5. $^-3 + {}^-7$

6. $^+3 + {}^-3$

7. $^+5 + {}^-6$

8. $^-1 + {}^+8$

_____

_____

_____

_____

9. $^-2 + {}^-6$

10. $^+4 + {}^-1$

11. $^-3 + {}^-7$

12. $^-2 + {}^+6$

_____

_____

_____

_____

13. $0 + {}^-6$

14. $^-5 + {}^+3$

15. $^-1 + {}^-9$

16. $^+4 + {}^-8$

_____

_____

_____

_____

17. $^-9 + {}^+6$

18. $^+9 + {}^-10$

19. $^-2 + {}^-2$

20. $^+1 + {}^-2$

_____

_____

_____

_____

Use two-color counters to find each sum. Then compare. Write >, <, or = .

21. $^-2 + {}^+5 \bigcirc {}^+3 + {}^-1$

22. $^-3 + {}^-6 \bigcirc {}^-6 + {}^-3$

23. $^+5 + {}^-1 \bigcirc {}^-5 + {}^+1$

24. $^-7 + {}^-2 \bigcirc {}^-3 + {}^-4$

25. $^+4 + {}^-5 \bigcirc {}^-8 + {}^+3$

26. $^-1 + {}^+1 \bigcirc {}^-1 + {}^-1$

Test Prep

27. On the first play of the football game, Curtis ran for a 5-yard gain. The next time he carried the ball, he was tackled in the backfield for a 9-yard loss. What was his total yardage on the two plays?

    A $^+14$

    C $^+4$

    B $^-4$

    D $^-14$

28. At the beginning of one dry season, the level of a certain African river was already 2 feet below normal. It dropped another 5 feet by the end of the season. The next year, the river level began the dry season 3 feet above normal, and dropped another 8 feet by the end of the season. Did the river reach a lower point in the first or the second year?

_____

Use with text pages 592–594.

Model Subtraction of Integers

Use two-color counters to find each difference.

1. $^-4 - {^+3}$ ____   2. $^+6 - {^+2}$ ____   3. $^-5 - {^-1}$ ____   4. $^+4 - {^-5}$ ____

5. $^-5 - {^-6}$ ____   6. $^+2 - {^+3}$ ____   7. $^+1 - {^-9}$ ____   8. $^-2 - {^+8}$ ____

9. $^+7 - {^+7}$ ____   10. $^+3 - {^-2}$ ____   11. $^-6 - {^-9}$ ____   12. $^-4 - {^+4}$ ____

13. $^+3 - {^-3}$ ____   14. $^-4 - {^+2}$ ____   15. $^-3 - {^-10}$ ____   16. $^+6 - {^-1}$ ____

17. $^-7 - {^+1}$ ____   18. $^+3 - {^-5}$ ____   19. $^-1 - {^-2}$ ____   20. $^+5 - {^-1}$ ____

Use two-color counters to find each difference. Then compare. Write $>$, $<$, or $=$.

21. $^+3 - {^-1} \bigcirc {^+4} - {^-2}$ 22. $^-5 - {^-9} \bigcirc {^+4} - {^+10}$ 23. $^+4 - {^-2} \bigcirc {^-4} - {^+2}$

24. $^-2 - {^-2} \bigcirc {^-9} - {^-9}$ 25. $^+7 - {^+4} \bigcirc {^-6} - {^-9}$ 26. $^-2 - {^+6} \bigcirc {^-7} - {^-1}$

Test Prep

27. During a recent dry spell, the water level in a local reservoir dropped 7 feet during July and another 4 feet during August. Which of the following shows how much the water level dropped during July and August?

   A $^-7 - {^-4}$ C $^+7 + {^+4}$

   B $^-7 + {^-4}$ D $^-4 - {^-7}$

28. Brian earned money shoveling snow in his neighborhood. He spent $5 on a book and $3 on a snack. How much less money did he have after he made his purchases? Express your answer as a negative integer.

   _____

Use with text pages 596–597.

Name _____ Date _____

Add and Subtract Integers

Decide whether the answer will be positive or negative. Then use the number line
to add or subtract.

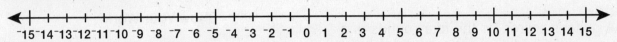

-15 -14 -13 -12 -11 -10 -9 -8 -7 -6 -5 -4 -3 -2 -1 0 1 2 3 4 5 6 7 8 9 10 11 12 13 14 15

1. $^+6 - {}^+4$ **2.** $^+7 - {}^-6$ **3.** $^-1 + {}^+6$ **4.** $^+6 + {}^-7$

_____   _____   _____   _____

5. $^-5 - {}^+3$ **6.** $^+1 - {}^-8$ **7.** $^+9 - {}^+2$ **8.** $^-2 - {}^+6$

_____   _____   _____   _____

9. $^-4 + {}^+2$ **10.** $^+8 - {}^+10$ **11.** $0 + {}^-1$ **12.** $^-8 - {}^-6$

_____   _____   _____   _____

13. $^+4 - {}^+5$ **14.** $^+3 + {}^-5$ **15.** $^-2 - {}^+3$ **16.** $^+1 + {}^-2$

_____   _____   _____   _____

17. $^-7 - {}^+3$ **18.** $^-8 + {}^-5$ **19.** $^+3 + {}^+4$ **20.** $^-4 - {}^-9$

_____   _____   _____   _____

Solve each equation. Use a number line to help you.

21. $^-15 + x = {}^-3$ **22.** $^+8 + x = {}^+6$ **23.** $x + {}^-5 = {}^-1$

_____   _____   _____

24. $x - {}^-8 = {}^+17$ **25.** $^-3 + x = {}^-9$ **26.** $x - {}^+7 = {}^-10$

_____   _____   _____

Test Prep

27. On Monday, the temperature at 7 P.M.
dropped 18 degrees below what it had
been the day before. On Tuesday, the
temperature at 7 P.M. was 14 degrees
warmer. What integer shows the overall
change in temperature from Sunday to
Tuesday?

_____

28. The highest average temperature in
Beijing, China is a very hot $^+30°C$. The
lowest average temperature is 38°C
colder than that. What is the lowest
average temperature for Beijing?

_____

        Use with text pages 598–600.

Problem-Solving Application:
Use Integers

Solve.

Show Your Work

1. A golfer's scores for the four rounds of a tournament were $^+4$, $^-3$, $^-2$, and $^-3$. What was the golfer's score after these four rounds?

   _____

2. Another golfer scored $^-2$, $^-5$, $^+3$, and $^-1$ for the four rounds. What was the golfer's score for the tournament?

   _____

3. During one round, another golfer's score on the first nine holes was $^+4$. What score does she have to have for the next nine holes to end the day at par, which is 0?

   _____

4. During a recent football game, Tyrell gained 6 yd, lost 4 yd, gained 2 yd, and lost 3 yd on each of his last two plays. How many yards did Tyrell gain or lose overall?

   _____

5. The temperature outside is $^-12°F$. The temperature increases by 8° and then goes down by 7°. What is the temperature?

   _____

Use with text pages 602–604.

Integers and the Coordinate Plane

Use the graph of the figures at the right
for Exercises 1–12. Write the ordered
pair for each point.

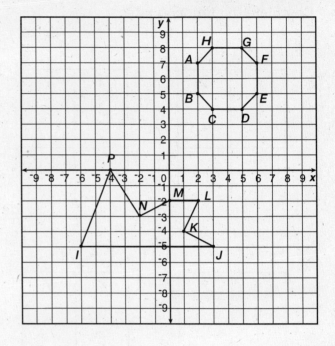

1. G _____   **2.** A _____

3. M _____   **4.** I _____

5. J _____   **6.** N _____

Write the letter name of each point.

7. $(^+2, {}^+5)$ _____   **8.** $(^+5, {}^+4)$ _____

9. $(^+2, {}^-2)$ _____   **10.** $(^-4, 0)$ _____

11. $(^+3, {}^+8)$ _____   **12.** $(^+1, {}^-4)$ _____

Use grid paper. Use the coordinates to plot the given points of figures.
Label each point with its letter.

13. $A\,(^-9, {}^-2)$ **14.** $B\,(^-4, {}^-5)$ **15.** $C\,(^-6, {}^+2)$ **16.** $D\,(^-3, 0)$ **17.** $E\,(0, {}^-3)$

18. $F\,(^+3, 0)$ **19.** $G\,(0, {}^+3)$ **20.** $H\,(^-5, {}^+3)$ **21.** $I\,(^-2, {}^-8)$ **22.** $J\,(^+4, {}^-4)$

23. $K\,(^+3, {}^-2)$ **24.** $L\,(^+8, {}^+1)$ **25.** $M\,(^+5, {}^+2)$ **26.** $N\,(^+7, {}^+3)$ **27.** $P\,(^+4, {}^+7)$

28. Connect points A–C in order. Connect C to A. Then connect points D–G
in order. Connect G to D. Then connect points H–P in order. Connect P to H.
What are the three figures you have drawn?

_____

✓ Test Prep

29. Write an ordered pair that would
appear in Quadrant I, in Quadrant II,
in Quadrant III, and in Quadrant IV.

_____   _____

_____   _____

30. Which ordered pair would appear
in Quadrant III?

A $(^+5, {}^+7)$ **C** $(^-5, {}^-7)$

B $(^-5, {}^+7)$ **D** $(^+5, {}^-7)$

Use with text pages 610–612.

Integers and Functions

Complete the function table.

1. $y = x + 8$

x	y
⁻2	
⁻1	
0	
⁺1	

2. $y = x - 4$

x	y
⁺1	
⁺2	
⁺3	
⁺4	

3. $y = 7x$

x	y
0	
6	
9	
12	

4. $y = 5 - x$

x	y
⁻2	
⁻1	
0	
⁺6	

5. $y = 2x + 1$

x	y
0	
1	
3	
4	

6. $y = 2 + x$

x	y
⁻3	
⁻2	
⁻1	
0	

7. $y = 3x - 6$

x	y
0	
⁺1	
⁺2	
⁺3	

8. $y = 4 - x$

x	y
⁺5	
⁺7	
⁺9	
⁺11	

9. The function $t = 65 - s$ expresses the temperature (t) in degrees Fahrenheit in a laboratory freezer for each second (s) of an experiment. What is the temperature after 84 seconds?

_____

10. The function $t = {}^-32 + s$ expresses the temperature (t) in degrees Fahrenheit in the freezer for each second (s) for another experiment. What is the temperature after 60 seconds?

_____

✓ Test Prep

11. Dana is raising a dairy cow for next summer's State Fair. At birth, Daisy, her Holstein heifer, weighed 31 pounds. Daisy should gain about 3 pounds each month. Dana lets m represent the number of months and uses the function $p = 31 + 3m$ to predict her heifer's future weight. How much should Daisy weigh in 2 months, 4 months, 6 months, and 8 months?

_____

12. Use the function $y = 2x - 15$ to find the value of y when $x = 4$.

A ⁻7

B ⁺7

C ⁻5

D ⁺5

Use with text pages 614–615.

Use Functions and Graphs

Find values of y to complete each function table.
Then graph each equation as a straight line on grid paper.

1. $y = x + 3$

x	y
-4	
-2	
0	
+2	

2. $y = x - 5$

x	y
-2	
-1	
0	
+1	

3. $y = 2x - 1$

x	y
0	
+1	
+2	
+3	

4. $y = 4x + 1$

x	y
0	
+2	
+4	
+6	

5. $y = 7x$

x	y
0	
+1	
+2	
+3	

6. $y = 6 + x$

x	y
-3	
-2	
-1	
0	

7. $y = 2x - 5$

x	y
0	
+1	
+2	
+3	

8. $y = 8 - x$

x	y
+1	
+2	
+4	
+6	

Find three ordered pairs for each function. Then use them
to graph the function as a straight line.

9. $y = x - 6$ _____

_____

10. $y = x + 2$ _____

_____

11. $y = x + 5$ _____

_____

12. $y = 6x$ _____

_____

13. $y = 3x$ _____

_____

14. $y = 5x$ _____

_____

15. $y = 3x - 2$ _____

_____

16. $y = 4x + 3$ _____

_____

17. $y = 5x - 1$ _____

_____

Test Prep

18. Graph $y = x$ and $y = 8x$ on the same
coordinate plane. How are the graphs
alike? How are they different?

_____

19. Find the ordered pair that is a solution
for $y = 5x + 5$.

A (4, 20)   **C** (2, 5)

B (0, 10)   **D** (4, 25)

Use with text pages 616–618.

Problem-Solving Application:
Use a Graph

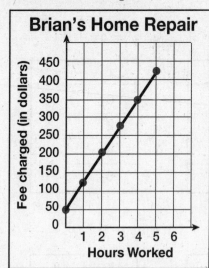

Brian's Home Repair

Fee charged (in dollars)

450
400
350
300
250
200
150
100
50
0

1 2 3 4 5 6
Hours Worked

Use the graph to solve Problems 1–5.

Show Your Work

1. How much does Brian charge for 2 hours of work?

   _____

2. How much of a fee does Brian charge for coming to the house to start work?

   _____

3. If you let c represent the fee Brian charges and h represent the number of hours he works, then the equation $c = 75h + 50$ represents this function. What points can be plotted to show the cost for each hour for hours 6, 7, and 8?

   _____

4. Ed needed to hire Brian for a job that lasted 2.5 hours. Ed wrote a check for $250. Was this the correct amount to pay? Explain.

   _____

   _____

5. Suppose Brian changes his rates and adds $15 to the cost of each hour. How would the equation and the graph change?

   _____

   _____

Use with text pages 620–621.

Name _____ Date _____

Transformations in the Coordinate Plane

Use the diagram. Name the coordinates of triangle *JKL* after the transformations.

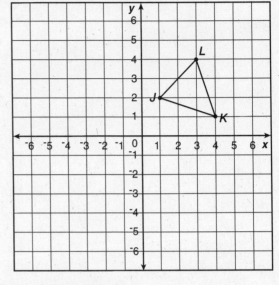

1. Translate left 4, then down 3.

2. Reflect over the *x*-axis.

3. Rotate 90° clockwise about (0, 0).

4. Reflect over the *y*-axis. Then rotate 270°
   counterclockwise around (0, 0).

Write *line, rotational,* or *both* to describe the symmetry of the figure.

5.
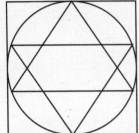
_____

6.
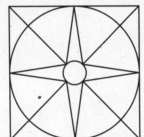
_____

7.
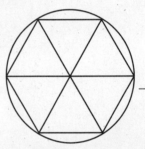
_____

8. A parallelogram was reflected across
the *y*-axis. It ended up at *A*(6, 1),
B(3, 1), *C*(1, 3), and *D*(4, 3). What
were the original coordinates of the
parallelogram?

_____

9. A triangle was translated left 6 and
down 3. It ended up at *A*($^-$5, 0),
B(0, $^-$1), and *C*($^-$1, 3). What were the
original coordinates of the triangle?

_____

Test Prep

10. Trapezoid *JKLM* has coordinates *J*(1, 2),
K(5, 2), *L*(5, 5), and *M*(2, 4). It was rotated
90°. What are its new coordinates?

_____

_____

11. Point *R*(4, $^-$3) is reflected across the
y-axis and then rotated 90°. What
are its new coordinates?

A (3, 4)   c ($^-$3, 4)

B (3, $^-$4)   D ($^-$3, $^-$4)

                   Use with text pages 622–624.